USDA

United States
Department of
Agriculture

Forest Service

**Northern
Research Station**

Resource Bulletin
NRS-42

Michigan Timber Industry: An Assessment of Timber Product Output and Use

2006

Ronald J. Piva
Anthony K. Weatherspoon

Abstract

Presents recent Michigan forest industry trends; production and receipts of industrial roundwood; and production of saw logs, veneer logs, pulpwood, and other products in 2006. Logging residue generated from timber harvest operations is reported, as well as wood and bark residue generated at primary wood-using mills and disposition of mill residues.

Cover Photo

Red pine stand next to clearcut. Phofo by Scott Pugh, U.S. Forest Service.

Contents

INTRODUCTION

Michigan's wood products manufacturing industry employs more than 28,000 workers with an output of approximately $6.7 billion (NAICS 321—Wood product manufacturing, and NAICS 322—Paper manufacturing) (U.S. Census Bureau 2002). Given the economic importance of the State's wood industry, the purpose of this bulletin is to analyze recent Michigan forest industry trends and report the results of a detailed study of the forest industry, industrial roundwood production, and associated primary mill wood and bark residue in Michigan in 2006. Such detailed information is necessary for intelligent planning and decisionmaking in wood procurement, economic research, forest resources management, and forest industry development. Likewise, researchers need current forest industry and industrial roundwood information for planning projects.

In 2004, the last detailed study of all industrial roundwood output in Michigan was released (Haugen and Weatherspoon 2010) and is used as a basis of comparison for most of this study's results. When new surveys are completed, errors and omissions from previous surveys are corrected. As a result of our ongoing efforts to improve the survey's efficiency and reliability, changes may have been made to the previous survey's data. All comparisons and analysis in this report are based on the reprocessed data from earlier surveys, which may not match earlier published data. Rows and columns of supporting tables may not sum due to rounding, but data in each table cell are accurately displayed.

Information about the forest land resource of Michigan is available at the Forest Inventory and Analysis Web site at: http://nrs.fs.fed.us/fia/data-tools/state-reports/MI

The Authors

RONALD J. PIVA, forester, received a B.S. in forest management from the University of Missouri-Columbia. He joined the Forest Service in 1987 and since then has been working with the Northern Research Station's Forest Inventory and Analysis Program. Corresponding author: rpiva@fs.fed.us, 651-649-5150

ANTHONY K. WEATHERSPOON, forest products specialist, received a B.S. in wood science and technology from Colorado State University and did graduate work in wood science there. He joined the Michigan Department of Natural Resources in 1985 and has been working there since.

STUDY METHODS

This study was a cooperative effort between the Michigan Department of Natural Resources (MI-DNR) and the Forest Inventory and Analysis (FIA) unit at the Northern Research Station (NRS) of the U.S. Forest Service. The FIA program is responsible for providing forest resource statistics for all ownerships across the United States, including timber products outputs.

Using questionnaires supplied by NRS and designed to determine the size and composition of the State's primary wood-using industry, its use of roundwood, and its generation and disposition of wood residues, MI-DNR surveyed all known primary wood-using mills. Completed questionnaires were sent to NRS to process and analyze. As part of data processing, all industrial roundwood volumes reported on the questionnaires were converted to standard units of measure using regional conversion factors. See Table 1 for conversion factors. Timber removals by source of material and harvest residues generated during logging were estimated from standard product volumes using factors developed from logging utilization studies previously conducted by NRS. Data on Michigan's industrial roundwood receipts were loaded into a regional timber removals database where they were supplemented with data on out-of state uses of Michigan roundwood to provide a complete assessment of Michigan's timber product output.

Certain terms used in this report—retained, export, import, production, and receipts—have specialized meanings and relationships unique to the FIA program that surveys timber product output (TPO) (Fig. 1).

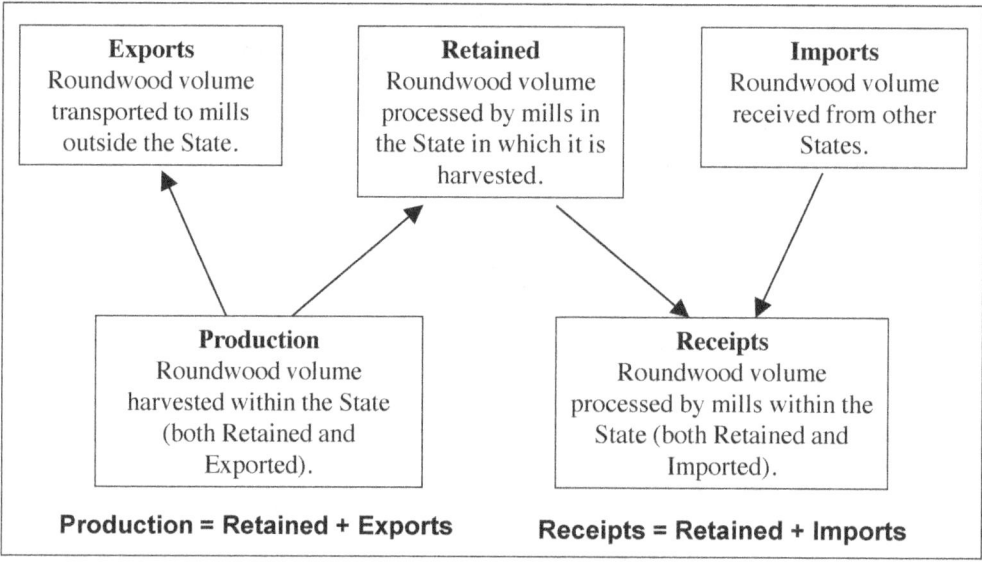

Figure 1.—Diagram of the movement of industrial roundwood.

Table 1.—Conversion factors from reported unit of measure to standard unit of measure[a]

Product and (Standard unit of measure)	Reported unit of measure							
	International ¼-inch rule MBF	Doyle scale MBF	Scribner Decimal C MBF	Green tons	Standard cord	Lake States cord	Thousand pieces	Thousand cubic feet
Saw logs (MBF International ¼-inch rule)	1	1.38	1.08	0.2174	0.5	0.52085		0.158
Veneer logs (MBF International ¼-inch rule)	1	1.14	1.04		0.5	0.52085		0.158
Pulp and composite products, and industrial fuelwood (Standard cords)				0.4167	1	1.0417		.079
Mine timbers (Thousand cubic feet)		0.2322	0.1817		0.079	0.0822943	6.7	1
Poles (Pieces)	20		21.6	4.348	10	10.4	1,000	0.0079
Posts (Thousand pieces)	0.2			0.04167	0.1	0.104	1	0.79
Cabin logs, excelsior/shavings, and miscellaneous products (Thousand cubic feet)	0.158	0.21804	0.17064	0.0329193	0.079	0.0822943	7.9	1

[a] Reported volume X conversion factor = Standard volume

PRIMARY TIMBER INDUSTRY IN MICHIGAN
Industrial roundwood

- In 2006, Michigan's primary wood-using industry included 206 sawmills, 5 veneer mills, 8 pulp and composite product mills, 7 cabin log mills, 6 industrial fuelwood mills, 12 post and pole mills, and 5 mills that produced other products (Table 2). There were 42 fewer medium and small sawmills in 2006 than in 2004.

- The Northern Lower Peninsula Forest Inventory Unit had 117 industrial roundwood processors in 2006, followed by the Southern Lower Peninsula unit with 71 industrial roundwood processors, the Eastern Upper Peninsula unit with 38, and the Western Upper Peninsula unit with 23 (Fig. 2).

- In 2006, the primary wood-using mills in Michigan processed 348.5 million cubic feet of industrial roundwood, a decrease of 5 percent from 2004 mills (Table 3).

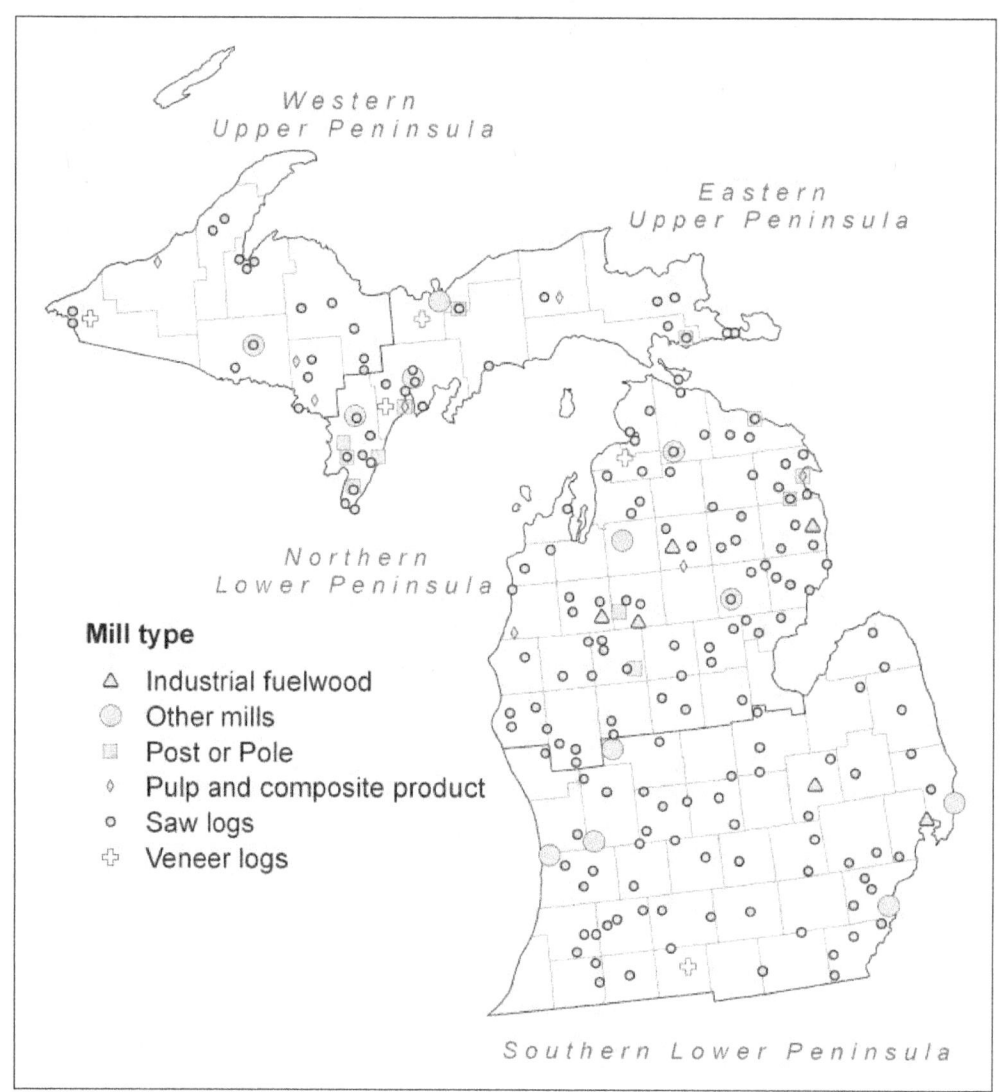

Figure 2.—Forest Inventory Units and location of wood-using mills, Michigan, 2006.

4

- Eighty-seven percent of the industrial roundwood processed by the State's primary wood-using mills in 2006 was cut from Michigan's forest lands. Wisconsin was the largest supplier of out-of-state wood for Michigan's forest products mills, supplying 10 percent of the total industrial roundwood processed (Table 4).

- Seventy-three percent of the industrial roundwood processed by Michigan's primary wood-using mills were hardwood species. Hard and soft maples, combined, accounted for 32 percent of the total volume processed. Other important species processed were aspen/balsam poplar, red pine, jack pine, and red oaks.

- Industrial roundwood production decreased by 7 percent, from 354.1 million cubic feet in 2004 to 329.9 million cubic feet in 2006 (Table 5 and Fig. 3). This decrease was mainly the result of the closure of pulp and composite panel mills in Michigan and Wisconsin in 2005 and 2006.

- Ninety-two percent of the 329.9 million cubic feet of industrial roundwood harvested in Michigan was processed by primary wood processors in the State (Table 6). Primary wood processors in Wisconsin received 55 percent of the industrial roundwood exported to other states. Other primary wood processors that processed industrial roundwood harvested in Michigan were located in Minnesota, Canada, Indiana, Ohio, Kentucky, Virginia, and other countries.

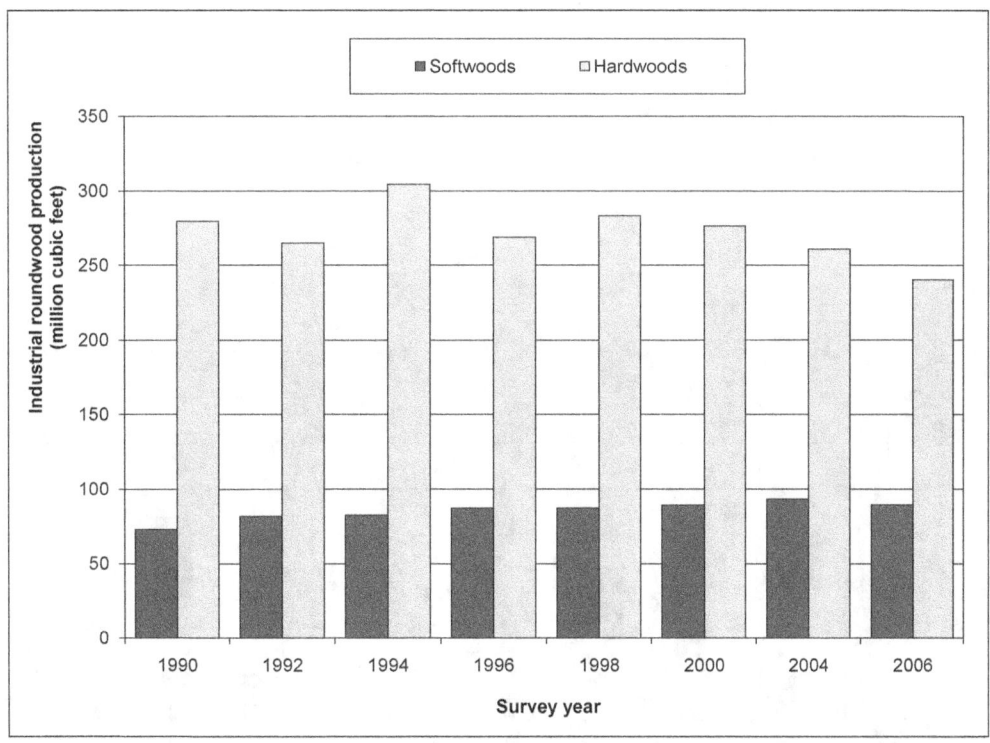

Figure 3.—Industrial roundwood production by softwoods and hardwoods, and survey year, Michigan (Hackett and Pilon 1993, May and Pilon 1995, Hackett and Pilon 1997, Haugen and Pilon 2002, Haugen and Weatherspoon 2003, Haugen and Weatherspoon 2010).

- In 2006, more than 40 percent (135.1 million cubic feet) of industrial roundwood was harvested from the Northern Lower Peninsula Forest Inventory Unit (Table 7). The Western Upper Peninsula Unit produced 96.6 million cubic feet of industrial roundwood followed by the Eastern Upper Unit at 73.1 million cubic feet, and the Southern Lower Peninsula Unit at 25.0 million cubic feet.

- Hard maple replaced aspen/balsam poplar as the most harvested species for industrial roundwood (Fig. 4). There was a 30-percent decrease in the volume of aspen harvested between 2004 and 2006. Most of this decrease was due to the loss of markets from the closing of pulp and composite products mills in Michigan and Wisconsin.

- Harvesting for pulpwood products accounted for almost half of the total industrial roundwood produced in 2006. Saw log mills were the second largest consumer of Michigan's industrial roundwood production, consuming almost 40 percent of the total production (Table 8 and Fig. 5).

Saw Logs

- Michigan's sawmills processed 765.7 million board feet of saw logs in 2006, an increase of 4 percent from 2004. Sawmills in the Northern Lower Peninsula Forest Inventory Unit processed 47 percent (374.6 million board feet) of the State's total saw log receipts (Table 9).

- Saw log production increased by 8 percent between 2004 and 2006, from 688.2 million board feet in 2004 to 741.3 million board feet.

- In 2006, red pine accounted for almost a quarter of the total harvest for saw logs from Michigan's forests. Other important species groups harvested were hard maple, red oaks, jack pine, soft maple, and aspen/balsam poplar (Fig. 6).

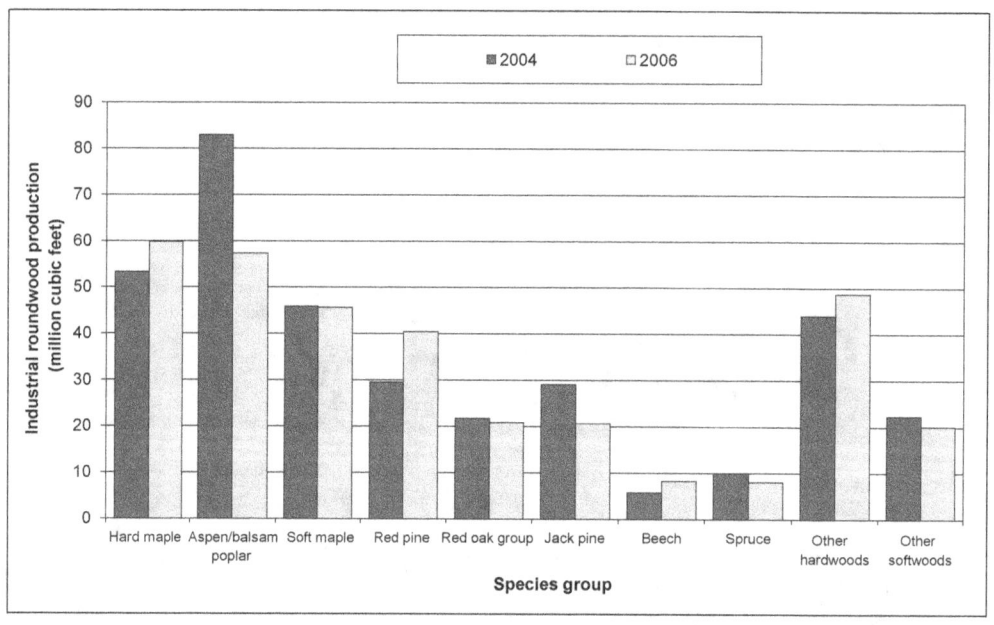

Figure 4.—Industrial roundwood production by species group, Michigan, 2004 and 2006.

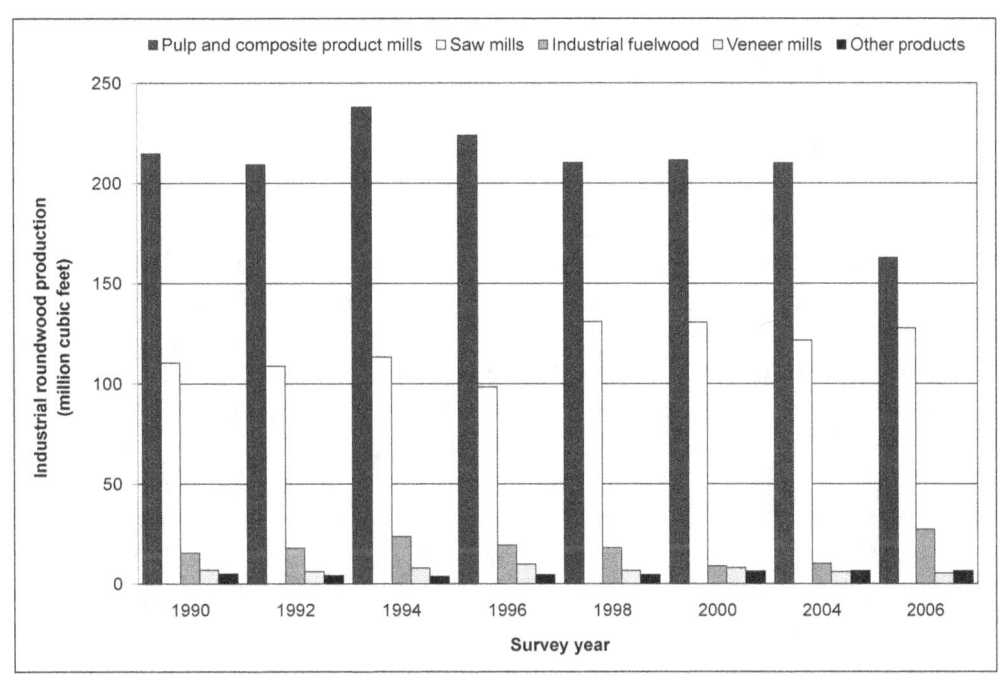

Figure 5.—Industrial roundwood production by product and survey year, Michigan (Hackett and Pilon 1993, May and Pilon 1995, Hackett and Pilon 1997, Haugen and Pilon 2002, Haugen and Weatherspoon 2003, Haugen and Weatherspoon 2010); 2000 data are from unpublished results.

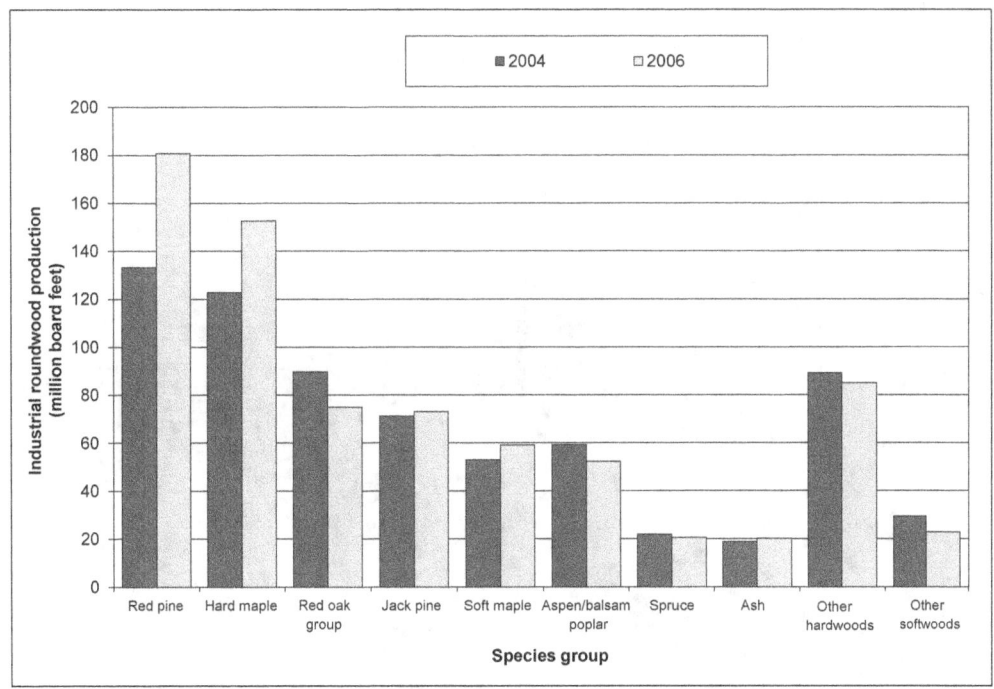

Figure 6.—Saw log production by species group, Michigan, 2004 and 2006.

Other Products

- Despite the 22-percent decrease in pulpwood production between 2004 and 2006, pulpwood remained the most harvested product from Michigan's forests in 2006 (Table 5). The results of a separate Northern Region pulpwood study conducted in 2006 are available (Piva 2010).

- Industrial fuelwood, the third most harvested product in Michigan in 2006, increased from 10.1 million cubic feet in 2004 to 27.4 million cubic feet in 2006.

- There was 33.2 million board feet of veneer harvested from Michigan in 2006. Hard maple, aspen/balsam poplar, and red oaks made up more than 75 percent of the total harvest.

- Other industrial roundwood products harvested from Michigan in 2006 were posts, poles, cabin logs, excelsior/shavings/mulch, and other miscellaneous products. Combined, these products made up only 2 percent of the total volume of industrial roundwood produced.

- Residential fuelwood is a major nonindustrial product in Michigan and is not included in this report. The results of a residential fuelwood study conducted in 1992 are available (May et. al. 1993).

Timber Removals

- During the harvest of industrial roundwood from Michigan's forests in 2006, 329.9 million cubic feet of wood material was used for primary wood products and another 96.6 million cubic feet of wood material was left on the ground as harvest residues (Table 10 and Fig. 7).

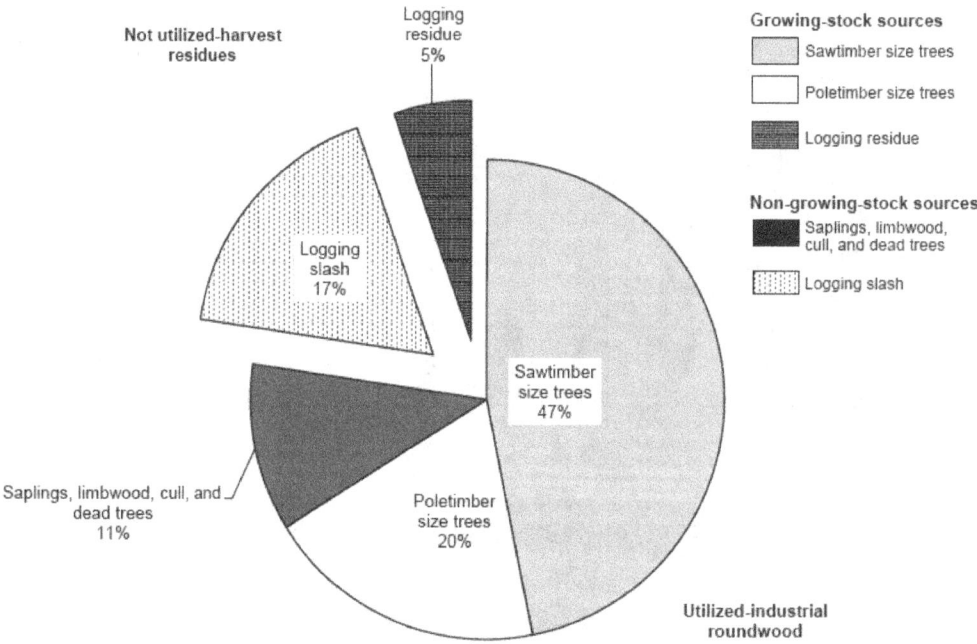

Figure 7.—Distribution of timber removals for industrial roundwood by source of material, Michigan, 2006.

- Growing-stock sources, at 304.3 million cubic feet, were the largest component of removals for industrial roundwood production. Ninety-three percent of the growing stock removed was used for products and 7 percent was left as harvest residue. Sawtimber-size trees accounted for 71 percent of the growing-stock volume that was used for products, and the remainder came from pole-size trees.

- In 2006, 122.3 million cubic feet of non-growing-stock wood material was removed in the production of industrial roundwood, but only 39 percent of this material was used for products, and the remainder was left on the ground as logging slash. Half of the non-growing-stock material used for industrial roundwood came from the limbs of growing-stock trees another 40 percent came from cull trees. The rest of the non-growing-stock material used for products came from dead trees and saplings.

- More than 40 percent of the total growing-stock material removed from Michigan's timberland in 2006 came from the Northern Lower Peninsula Forest Inventory Unit (Table 11), followed by the Western Upper Peninsula Unit with 29 percent of the total growing-stock volume removed, the Eastern Upper Peninsula Unit with 22 percent, and the Southern Lower Peninsula Unit with 8 percent.

- In 2006, 1.1 billion board feet was removed from Michigan's sawtimber inventory on timberland (Table 12). Hard maple, red pine, and aspen/balsam poplar accounted for half of the total sawtimber volume removed.

- The harvesting of industrial roundwood products from Michigan's forests in 2006 left 96.6 million cubic feet of harvest residues on the ground (Table 13). About two-thirds of the harvest residues produced were in the Northern Lower Peninsula unit (33.6 million cubic feet) and the Western Upper Peninsula unit (32.1 million cubic feet).

Harvest Intensity

- Statewide in 2006, there was an average of 22 cubic feet of total wood material removed per acre of forest land in Michigan. Only 11 counties had more that 30 cubic feet of total wood material removed per acre of forest land (Fig. 8). (For reference, a cord of roundwood contains about 80 cubic feet of wood.)

- In 2006, there were 19.5 million acres of forest land in Michigan (Pugh 2007). The net volume in live trees on forest land was 31.1 billion cubic feet. The average volume of live trees per acre in Michigan in 2006 was 1,590 cubic feet per acre. The 426.5 million cubic feet of total wood material removed due to harvesting (Table 10) was less than 1½ percent of the total live volume of trees on forest land in Michigan.

- The Western Upper Peninsula Forest Inventory Unit had the greatest harvest intensity in 2006, with an average of 26 cubic feet of total wood removals per acre of forest land. The Eastern Upper Peninsula Unit had 24 cubic feet of total wood removals per acre of forest land followed by the Northern Lower Peninsula Unit with 23 cubic feet, and the Southern Lower Peninsula Unit with 1 cubic foot.

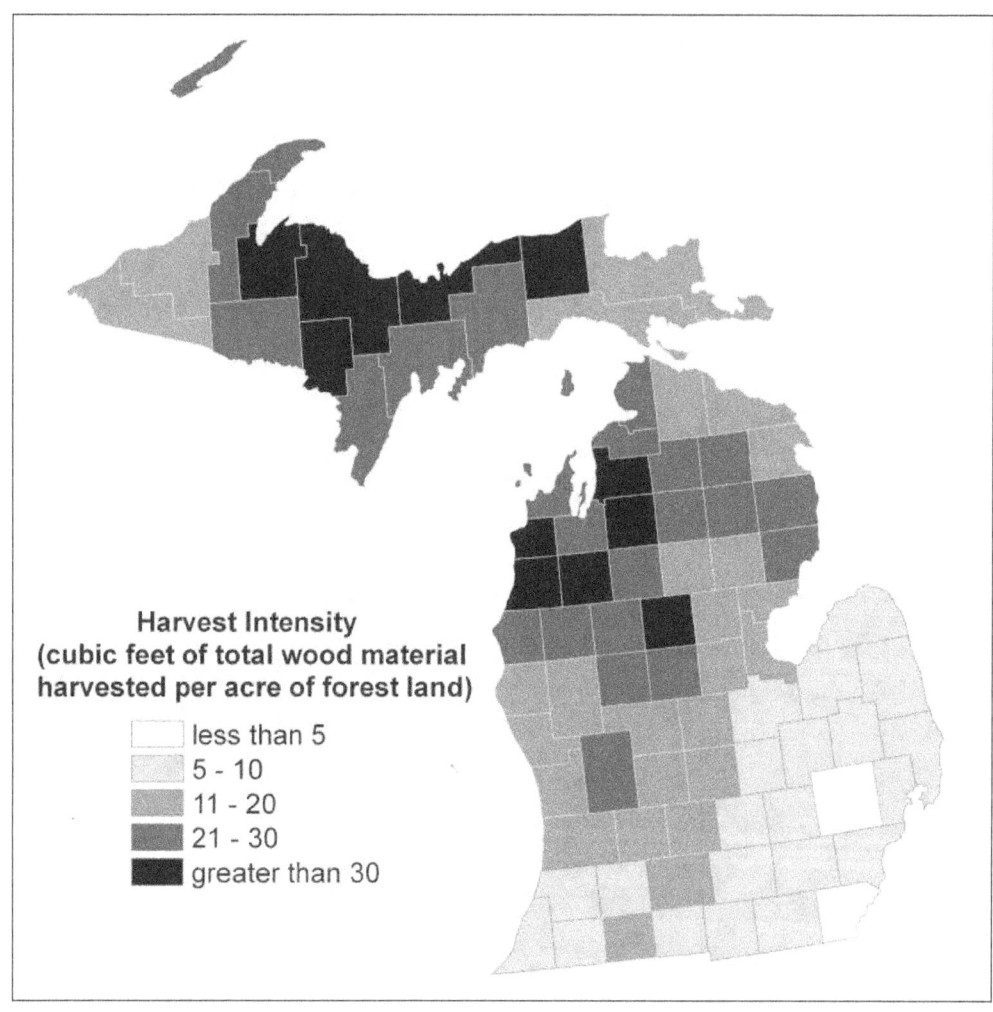

Figure 8.—Harvest intensity for industrial roundwood production, Michigan, 2006.

Primary Mill Residues

- In converting industrial roundwood into products, such as lumber, wood pulp, and veneer, Michigan's primary wood-using industries generated 3.0 million green tons of wood residue (coarse and fine residues) and bark residue (Table 14).

- Thirty-seven percent of the mill residues were in the form of coarse wood residue, such as slabs and edgings. Bark residue made up another 36 percent of the total mill residues produced, and fine residue accounted for the remaining 27 percent (Fig. 9).

- Forty-six percent of the mill residues generated were used for industrial fuelwood. Pulp and composite product mills consumed 32 percent of the mill residues; miscellaneous uses, such as livestock bedding, mulch, and small dimension lumber, consumed 19 percent; and residential fuelwood consumed 2 percent of the mill residues generated. Only 1 percent of the mill residues generated by the primary wood processors of Michigan went unused (Fig. 10).

- Seventy-three percent of the coarse residue was used by pulp and composite panel mills. Industrial fuelwood consumed 56 percent of the total fine residue generated and 69 percent of the bark residue generated in 2006.

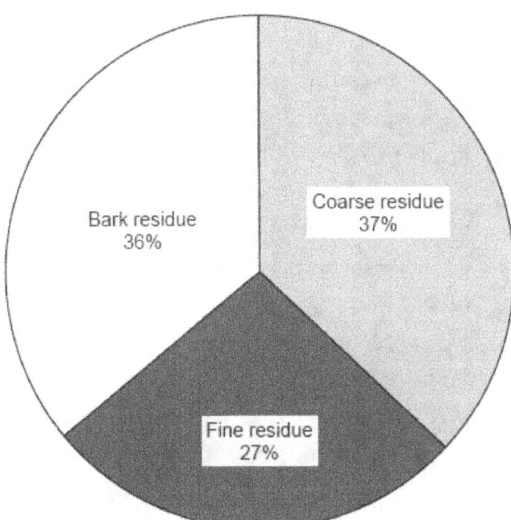

Figure 9.—Distribution of residues generated by primary wood-using mills by type of residue, Michigan, 2006.

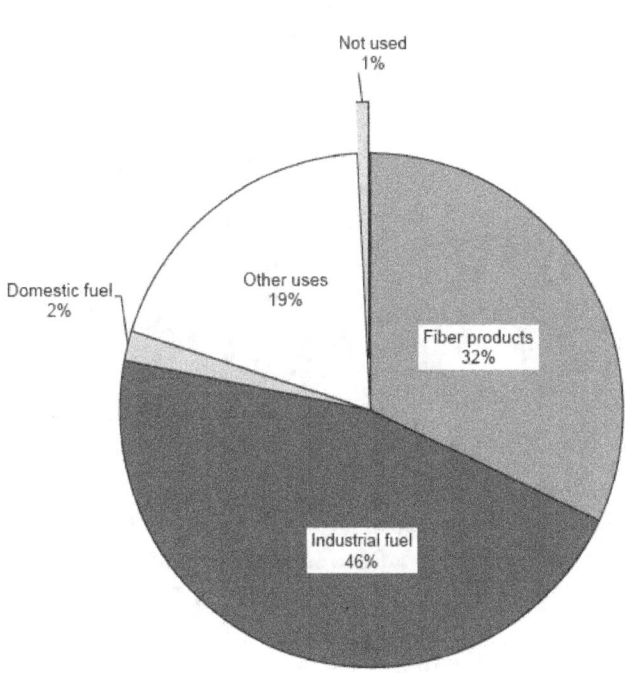

Figure 10.—Distribution of residues generated by primary wood-using mills by method of disposal, Michigan, 2006.

ACKNOWLEDGMENTS

Special thanks are given to the primary wood-using firms for supplying information for this study and to the Michigan Department of Natural Resources whose cooperation in canvassing survey respondents is greatly appreciated.

Figures 2 and 8 were created by Dale Gormanson, forester with Forest Inventory and Analysis in St. Paul, MN.

LITERATURE CITED

Hackett, Ronald L.; Pilon, John. 1993. **Michigan timber industry—an assessment of timber product output and use, 1990.** Resour. Bull. NC-144. St. Paul, MN: U.S. Department of Agriculture, Forest Service, North Central Forest Experiment Station. 56 p.

Hackett, Ronald L.; Pilon, John. 1997. **Michigan timber industry—an assessment of timber product output and use, 1994.** Resour. Bull. NC-189. St. Paul, MN: U.S. Department of Agriculture, Forest Service, North Central Forest Experiment Station. 66 p.

Haugen, David E.; Pilon, John. 2002. **Michigan timber industy—an assessment of timber product output and use, 1996.** Resour. Bull. NC-203. St. Paul, MN: U.S. Department of Agriculture, Forest Service, North Central Forest Experiment Station. 85 p.

Haugen, David E.; Weatherspoon, Anthony. 2003. **Michigan timber industry—an assessment of timber product output and use, 1998.** Resour. Bull. NC-212. St. Paul, MN: U.S. Department of Agriculture, Forest Service, North Central Research Station. 83 p.

Haugen, David E.; Weatherspoon, Anthony K. 2010. **Michigan timber industry—an assessment of timber product output and use, 2004.** Resour. Bull. NRS-40. Newtown Square, PA: U.S. Department of Agriculture, Forest Service, Northern Research Station. 91 p. [Available only online at: http://nrs.fs.fed.us/pubs/35581].

May, Dennis M.; Pilon, John. 1995. **Michigan timber industry—an assessment of timber product output and use, 1992.** Resour. Bull. NC-162. St. Paul, MN: U.S. Department of Agriculture, Forest Service, North Central Forest Experiment Station. 64 p.

May, Dennis M.; Weatherspoon, Anthony K.; Hackett, Ronald L. 1993. **Residential fuelwood consumption and production in Michigan, 1992.** Resour. Bull. NC-148. St. Paul, MN: U.S. Department of Agriculture, Forest Service, North Central Forest Experiment Station. 29 p.

Piva, Ronald J. 2010. **Pulpwood production in the northern region, 2006.** Resour. Bull. NRS-38. Newtown Square, PA: U.S. Department of Agriculture, Forest Service, Northern Research Station. 104 p.

Pugh, S.A. 2007. **Michigan's forest resources, 2006.** Research Note NRS-6. Newtown Square, PA: U.S. Department of Agriculture, Forest Service, Northern Research Station. 4 p. [Available only online at: http://nrs.fs.fed.us/pubs/2491].

U. S. Census Bureau. 2002. **2002 Economic Census – Manufacturing - Michigan.** Retrieved November 20, 2009, from http://www.census.gov/econ/census02/data/mi/MI000_31.HTM

DEFINITION OF TERMS

Board foot. Unit of measure applied to roundwood. It relates to lumber that is 1 foot long, 1 foot wide, and 1 inch thick (or its equivalent).

Bolt. A short log no more than 8 feet long, to be sawn for lumber, peeled or sliced for veneer, shaved for excelsior, or converted into shingles, cooperage stock, dimension stock, blocks, blanks, or other products.

Central stem. The portion of a tree between a 1-foot stump and the minimum 4.0-inch top diameter outside bark, or point where the central stem breaks into limbs.

Coarse mill residue. Wood residue suitable for chipping such as slabs, edgings, and veneer cores.

Commercial species. Tree species presently or prospectively suitable for industrial wood products. (Note: Excludes species of typically small size, poor form, or inferior quality such as hophornbeam, Osage-orange, and redbud.)

Cull removals. Net volume of rough and rotten trees plus the net volume in sections of the central stem of growing-stock trees that do not meet regional merchantability standards but are harvested for industrial roundwood products.

Diameter at breast height (d.b.h.). The outside bark diameter at 4.5 feet above the forest floor on the uphill side of the tree. For determining breast height, the forest floor includes the duff layer that may be present, but does not include unincorporated woody debris that may rise above the ground line.

Doyle rule. A simple log rule or formula for estimating the board-foot volume of logs based on a 4-inch slabbing allowance to square the log. This rule is used in the Eastern and Southern United States.

Exports. The volume of roundwood utilized by mills outside the state where the timber was harvested.

Fine mill residue. Wood residue not suitable for chipping, such as sawdust and veneer clippings.

Forest land. Land at least 10-percent stocked with trees of any size, or formerly having had such tree cover, and not currently developed for nonforest use. (Note: Stocking is measured by comparing specified standards with basal area and/or number of trees, age or size, and spacing.) The minimum area for classification of forest land is 1 acre. Roadside, streamside, and shelterbelt strips of timber must have a crown width of at least 120 feet to qualify as forest land. Unimproved roads and trails, streams or other bodies of water, or clearings in forest areas shall be classified as forest if less than 120 feet wide.

Growing-stock removals. The growing-stock volume removed from timberland by harvesting industrial roundwood products. (Note: Includes sawtimber removals, poletimber removals, and logging residues.)

Growing-stock tree. A live timberland tree of commercial species that meets specified standards of size, quality, and merchantability. (Note: Excludes rough, rotten, and dead trees.)

Growing-stock volume. Net volume of growing-stock trees 5.0 inches d.b.h. and larger, from 1 foot above the ground to a minimum 4.0-inch top diameter outside bark of the central stem or to the point where the central stem breaks into limbs.

Hardwoods. Dicotyledonous trees, usually broad-leaved and deciduous.

Harvest residues. The total net volume of unused portions of trees cut or killed by logging. (Note: Includes both logging residues and logging slash.)

Industrial fuelwood. A roundwood product, with or without bark, used to generate energy at manufacturing facilities and schools, correctional institutions, or electric generating plants.

Imports. The volume of roundwood delivered to a mill or group of mills in a specific state but harvested outside that state.

Industrial roundwood exports. The quantity of industrial roundwood harvested in a geographical area and transported to other geographical areas.

Industrial roundwood imports. The quantity of industrial roundwood received from other geographical areas.

Industrial roundwood products. Saw logs, pulpwood, veneer logs, poles, commercial posts, pilings, cooperage logs, particleboard bolts, shaving bolts, lath bolts, charcoal bolts, and chips from roundwood used for pulp or board products.

Industrial roundwood production. The quantity of industrial roundwood harvested in a geographic area plus all industrial roundwood exported to other geographical areas.

Industrial roundwood receipts. The quantity of industrial roundwood received by commercial mills in a geographic area plus all industrial roundwood imported from other geographical areas.

Industrial roundwood retained. The quantity of industrial roundwood harvested from and processed by commercial mills within the same geographical area.

International 1/4-inch rule. A log rule or formula for estimating the board-foot volume of logs, allowing ½ inch of taper for each 4-foot length, and assuming ¼ inch of kerf. This rule is used as the U.S. Forest Service standard log rule in the Eastern United States.

Limbwood removals. Net volume of all portions of a tree other than the central stem (including forks, large limbs, tops, and stumps) harvested for industrial roundwood products.

Logging residue. The net volume of unused portions of the merchantable central stem of growing-stock trees cut or killed by logging.

Logging slash. The net volume of unused portions of the unmerchantable (non-growing stock) sections of trees cut or killed by logging.

Merchantable sections. Refers to sections of the central stem of growing-stock trees that meet either pulpwood or saw log specifications.

Net volume. Gross volume less deductions for rot, sweep, or other defects affecting use for roundwood products.

Noncommercial species. Trees species of typically small size, poor form, or inferior quality that normally do not develop into trees suitable for industrial roundwood products. Noncommercial species are listed in the volume tables as rough trees.

Nonforest land. Land that has never supported forests, and land formerly forested where use for timber management is precluded by development for other uses. (Note: Includes areas used for crops, active Christmas tree plantations, orchards, nurseries, improved pasture, residential areas, city parks, improved roads of any width and adjoining clearings, powerline clearings of any width, and 1- to 39.9-acre areas of water classified by the Bureau of the Census as land.) If intermingled in forest areas, unimproved roads and nonforest strips must be more than 120 feet wide and more than 1 acre to qualify as nonforest land.

Nonforest land removals. Net volume of trees on nonforest lands harvested for industrial roundwood products.

Poletimber. A growing-stock tree at least 5.0 inches d.b.h. but smaller than sawtimber size (9.0 inches d.b.h. for softwoods, 11.0 inches d.b.h. for hardwoods).

Poletimber removals. Net volume in the merchantable central stem of poletimber trees harvested for industrial roundwood products.

Primary wood-using mills. Mills receiving roundwood or chips from roundwood for processing into products such as lumber, veneer, and pulp.

Primary wood-using mill residue. Wood materials (coarse and fine) and bark generated at manufacturing plants that process industrial roundwood into principal products. These residues include wood products obtained incidental to production of principal products and wood materials not utilized for some product.

Production. The quantity of roundwood material harvested in a geographic area plus all roundwood material exported to other geographical areas.

Receipts. The quantity of roundwood material received by commercial mills in a geographic area plus all roundwood material imported from other geographical areas.

Retained. Roundwood volume harvested from and processed by mills within the same state.

Rotten tree. A tree that does not meet regional merchantability standards because of excessive unsound cull.

Rough tree. A tree that does not meet regional merchantability standards because of excessive sound cull (includes forks, sweep and crook, and large branches or knots), including noncommercial tree species.

Roundwood. Logs, bolts, or other round sections cut from trees (including chips from roundwood).

Sapling. A live tree between 1.0 and 5.0 inches d.b.h.

Saw log portion. That portion of the central stem of sawtimber trees between the stump and the saw log top.

Saw log top. The point on the central stem of sawtimber trees above which a saw log cannot be produced. The minimum saw log top is 7.0 inches diameter outside bark for softwoods and 9.0 inches diameter outside bark for hardwoods.

Sawtimber removals. As used in Table 10, sawtimber removals refers to the net volume in the merchantable central stem of sawtimber-size trees harvested for industrial roundwood products. (Note: includes the saw log and upper stem portions of sawtimber-size trees.) When referring to the sawtimber volume removed from timberland as in Table 12, sawtimber removals refers to the net volume in the saw log portion of sawtimber-size trees harvested for roundwood products or left on the ground as harvest residue, and is usually expressed in thousands of board feet (International 1/4-inch rule).

Sawtimber tree. A growing-stock tree containing at least a 12-foot saw log or two noncontiguous saw logs 8 feet or longer, and meeting regional specifications for freedom from defect. Softwoods must be at least 9.0 inches d.b.h. and hardwoods must be at least 11.0 inches d.b.h.

Sawtimber volume. Net volume in the saw log portion of sawtimber trees.

Softwoods. Coniferous trees, usually evergreen, having needles or scale-like leaves.

Timber product output. The volume of roundwood products produced from an area's forests.

Timberland. Forest land that is producing, or is capable of producing, in excess of 20 cubic feet per acre per year of industrial roundwood products under natural conditions, is not withdrawn from timber utilization by statute or administrative regulation, and is not associated with urban or rural development.

Tree. A woody perennial plant, typically large, with a single well-defined stem carrying a more or less definite crown; sometimes defined as attaining a minimum diameter of 3 in. (7.6 cm) and a minimum height of 15 ft (4.6 m) at maturity. For FIA, any plant on the tree list in the current field manual is measured as a tree.

Upper stem portion. That portion of the central stem of sawtimber trees between the saw log top and the minimum top diameter of 4.0 inches outside bark, or to the point where the central stem breaks into limbs.

COMMON AND SCIENTIFIC NAMES OF TREE SPECIES BY SPECIES GROUP

Softwoods

Cedars
    Eastern redcedar   *Juniperus virginiana*
    Northern white-cedar   *Thuja occidentalis*
Balsam fir   *Abies balsamea*
Eastern hemlock   *Tsuga canadensis*
Tamarack   *Larix laricina*
Jack pine   *Pinus banksiana*
Shortleaf pine   *Pinus echinata*
Loblolly pine   *Pinus taeda*
Red pine   *Pinus resinosa*
White pine   *Pinus strobus*
Other pines
    Scotch pine   *Pinus sylvestris*
    Austrian pine   *Pinus nigra*
Spruce
    Norway spruce   *Picea abies*
    White spruce   *Picea glauca*
    Black spruce   *Picea mariana*
    Blue spruce   *Picea pungens*

Hardwoods

Ash
    White ash   *Fraxinus americana*
    Black ash   *Fraxinus nigra*
    Green ash   *Fraxinus pennsylvanica*
    Blue ash   *Fraxinus quadrangulata*
Aspen/balsam poplar
    Balsam poplar   *Populus balsamifera*
    Bigtooth aspen   *Populus grandidentata*
    Quaking aspen   *Populus tremuloides*
American basswood   *Tilia americana*
American beech   *Fagus grandifolia*
Yellow birch   *Betula alleghaniensis*
White birch   *Betula papyrifera*
Other birches
    River birch   *Betula nigra*
Black cherry   *Prunus serotina*
Black walnut   *Juglans nigra*
Eastern cottonwood   *Populus deltoides*
Elm
    American elm   *Ulmus americana*
    Siberian elm   *Ulmus pumila*

Slippery elm	*Ulmus rubra*
Rock elm	*Ulmus thomasii*
Hickory	
Mockernut hickory	*Carya alba*
Bitternut hickory	*Carya cordiformis*
Pignut hickory	*Carya glabra*
Shellbark hickory	*Carya laciniosa*
Shagbark hickory	*Carya ovata*
Hard maples	
Black maple	*Acer nigrum*
Sugar maple	*Acer saccharum*
Soft maples	
Boxelder	*Acer negundo*
Red maple	*Acer rubrum*
Silver maple	*Acer saccharinum*
Red oak group	
Scarlet oak	*Quercus coccinea*
Northern pin oak	*Quercus ellipsoidalis*
Pin oak	*Quercus palustris*
Northern red oak	*Quercus rubra*
Black oak	*Quercus velutina*
White oak group	
White oak	*Quercus alba*
Swamp white oak	*Quercus bicolor*
Bur oak	*Quercus macrocarpa*
Chinkapin oak	*Quercus muehlenbergii*
Chestnut oak	*Quercus prinus*
Sweetgum	*Liquidambar styraciflua*
American sycamore	*Platanus occidentalis*
Yellow-poplar	*Liriodendron tulipifera*
Other hardwoods	
Ohio buckeye	*Aesculus glabra*
Northern catalpa	*Catalpa speciosa*
Hackberry	*Celtis occidentalis*
Flowering dogwood	*Cornus florida*
Honeylocust	*Gleditsia triacanthos*
Kentucky coffeetree	*Gymnocladus dioicus*
Butternut	*Juglans cinerea*
White mulberry	*Morus alba*
Red mulberry	*Morus rubra*
Pin cherry	*Prunus pensylvanica*
Chokecherry	*Prunus virginiana*
Black locust	*Robinia pseudoacacia*
White willow	*Salix alba*
Black willow	*Salix nigra*
Sassafras	*Sassafras albidum*

TABLES

Table 2. -- Number of active primary wood-using mills by mill type and survey year, Michigan[a]

Kind of mill and mill size		Survey Year							
		1990	1992	1994	1996	1998	2000	2004	2006
Sawmills	Large[b]	39	29	33	27	34	34	36	38
	Medium[c]	105	106	97	94	95	74	83	61
	Small[d]	200	179	145	152	139	138	127	107
	Total	344	314	275	273	268	246	246	206
Veneer mills		7	7	5	4	5	5	4	4
Pulp and composite product mills		11	11	11	12	12	12	12	8
Industrial fuelwood[e]		8	7	9	5	6	5	4	6
Post and pole mills		19	7	7	10	14	11	10	12
Other products[f]		16	9	8	14	16	15	12	12
All mills		405	355	315	318	321	294	288	248

[a] Mills that produce more than one product are counted only for the product they process the most of.

[b] Annual lumber production in excess of 5 million board feet.

[c] Annual lumber production from 1 million to 5 million board feet.

[d] Annual lumber production less than 1 million board feet.

[e] Does not include residential fuelwood.

[f] Includes plants producing mulch, mine timbers, excelsior, shavings, etc.

Table 3.--Industrial roundwood receipts by mill type, hardwoods and softwoods, and survey year, Michigan

(In thousand cubic feet)

ALL SPECIES

Kind of mill	Survey Year							
	1990	1992	1994	1996	1998	2000	2004	2006
Saw mills	99,358.5	100,029.3	102,916.8	90,751.8	126,321.4	129,850.6	129,811.2	132,727.1
Veneer mills	6,783.8	6,519.0	7,204.7	8,653.7	5,946.8	9,389.7	6,455.4	6,378.4
Pulp and composite product mills	207,623.3	200,609.7	235,654.4	222,370.4	212,920.9	215,122.5	214,318.5	175,543.5
Cabin log mills	1,224.0	978.0	649.0	1,117.2	1,572.3	1,850.9	1,375.8	254.4
Industrial fuelwood[a]	15,445.1	18,029.6	23,798.7	19,372.3	18,107.3	8,869.8	10,088.3	27,359.0
Post and poles	2,868.7	3,030.4	2,412.2	2,948.7	2,478.2	3,844.2	4,394.9	5,731.1
Other products[b]	1,304.0	51.5	23.8	13.4	49.6	7.6	738.0	507.4
Total	334,607.5	329,247.6	372,659.7	345,227.5	367,396.5	368,935.5	367,182.1	348,500.9

SOFTWOODS

	1990	1992	1994	1996	1998	2000	2004	2006
Saw mills	21,319.7	22,583.0	22,132.8	21,053.1	35,635.3	46,134.4	58,679.5	60,009.3
Veneer mills	1,788.5	470.3	406.8	466.2	697.9	835.8	651.2	888.6
Pulp and composite product mills	29,790.2	33,064.5	33,534.7	37,651.9	34,754.2	34,633.7	34,672.3	21,182.5
Cabin log mills	1,224.0	978.0	649.0	1,117.2	1,549.3	1,850.9	1,375.8	252.2
Industrial fuelwood[a]	2,976.1	8,655.8	7,776.9	12,621.9	6,649.1	2,553.8	2,284.3	6,473.3
Post and poles	2,868.7	3,030.4	2,392.2	2,328.7	2,455.8	3,844.2	4,394.9	5,731.1
Other products[b]	16.0	47.8	20.2	13.4	16.9	3.6	2.1	41.5
Total	59,983.2	68,829.9	66,912.6	75,252.5	81,758.5	89,856.5	102,060.1	94,578.5

HARDWOODS

	1990	1992	1994	1996	1998	2000	2004	2006
Saw mills	78,038.8	77,446.3	80,784.0	69,698.7	90,686.2	83,716.2	71,131.6	72,717.8
Veneer mills	4,995.3	6,048.8	6,797.9	8,187.5	5,248.9	8,553.9	5,804.2	5,489.8
Pulp and composite product mills	177,833.1	167,545.2	202,119.8	184,718.5	178,166.7	180,488.8	179,646.2	154,361.0
Cabin log mills	--	--	--	--	23.0	--	--	2.2
Industrial fuelwood[a]	12,469.0	9,373.8	16,021.8	6,750.3	11,458.1	6,316.0	7,804.1	20,885.6
Post and poles	0.0	0.0	20.0	620.0	22.4	0.0	0.0	0.0
Other products[b]	1,288.0	3.6	3.6	0.0	32.8	4.0	735.9	466.0
Total	274,624.3	260,417.7	305,747.1	269,975.0	285,638.1	279,078.9	265,122.0	253,922.4

[a] Does not include residential fuelwood.
[b] Includes plants producing mulch, mine timbers, excelsior, shavings, etc.
All table cells without observations are indicated by --. Table value of 0.0 indicates the volume rounds to less than 0.1 thousand cubic feet. Columns and rows may not add to their totals due to rounding.

Table 4. -- Industrial roundwood receipts by Forest Inventory Unit, species group, and State of origin, Michigan, 2006

(In thousand cubic feet)

ALL UNITS

Species group	Total					State of origin							
		Illinois	Indiana	Iowa	Kentucky	Michigan	Minnesota	New York	Pennsylvania	Tennessee	Wisconsin	Other U.S.	Canada
Softwoods													
Eastern redcedar	10	--	--	--	--	10	--	--	--	--	--	--	--
Northern white-cedar	4,860	--	--	--	--	4,602	--	--	--	--	137	--	120
Balsam fir	5,646	--	--	--	--	5,029	--	--	--	--	614	--	3
Hemlock	4,865	--	--	--	--	4,478	--	--	--	--	386	--	1
Jack pine	24,103	--	--	--	--	19,543	--	--	--	--	4,558	--	2
Loblolly/shortleaf pine	32	--	--	--	--	--	--	--	--	--	--	32	--
Red pine	43,539	--	--	--	--	39,777	33	--	--	--	3,682	0	46
White pine	3,197	--	--	--	--	3,080	--	--	--	--	116	--	0
Other pine	302	--	--	--	--	302	--	--	--	--	--	--	--
Spruce	6,870	--	--	--	--	5,382	--	--	--	--	1,381	--	106
Tamarack	1,155	--	--	--	--	947	--	--	--	--	207	--	0
Total	94,579	--	--	--	--	83,151	33	--	--	--	11,081	33	280
Hardwoods													
Ash	6,980	--	--	--	--	6,433	--	--	--	--	441	1	105
Aspen/balsam poplar	58,699	--	--	--	--	53,938	16	--	--	--	2,847	--	1,897
Basswood	7,788	--	0	--	--	6,774	--	--	--	--	928	--	87
Beech	9,020	--	--	--	--	7,825	--	--	--	--	787	--	408
White birch	7,390	--	--	--	--	5,913	--	4	--	--	1,156	--	318
Yellow birch	4,388	--	--	--	--	3,501	--	9	--	--	640	--	237
Black cherry	3,132	--	3	--	--	3,019	--	1	63	--	12	1	33
Black walnut	701	18	21	--	18	601	--	--	--	21	--	1	--
Cottonwood	293	--	--	--	--	292	--	--	--	--	--	0	--
Elm	382	--	0	--	--	381	--	--	--	--	--	--	0
Hickory	470	2	7	--	5	453	--	2	--	--	--	0	--
Hard maple	63,863	--	33	--	--	54,745	--	124	18	--	6,048	4	2,892
Soft maple	48,299	--	3	--	--	41,152	--	3	--	--	5,226	--	1,915
Red oak group	20,438	--	7	--	--	18,835	--	0	151	--	1,286	0	158
White oak group	4,444	50	50	--	83	4,144	--	--	--	58	--	1	--
Sycamore	117	--	--	--	--	117	--	--	--	--	--	--	--
Yellow-poplar	88	--	7	--	--	81	--	--	--	--	--	--	--
Other hardwoods	17,431	--	--	--	--	12,532	--	--	--	--	4,724	--	174
Total	253,922	70	132	--	102	220,735	16	142	232	81	24,096	10	8,224
State total	348,501	70	132	--	102	303,886	49	142	232	81	35,177	43	8,504

(Table 4 continued)

EASTERN UPPER PENINSULA

		State of origin											
Species group	Total	Illinois	Indiana	Iowa	Kentucky	Michigan	Minnesota	New York	Pennsylvania	Tennessee	Wisconsin	Other U.S.	Canada
Softwoods													
Northern white-cedar	3,524	---	---	---	---	3,266	---	---	---	---	137	---	120
Balsam fir	3,116	---	---	---	---	3,035	---	---	---	---	79	---	3
Hemlock	4,608	---	---	---	---	4,221	---	---	---	---	386	---	1
Jack pine	3,513	---	---	---	---	3,473	---	---	---	---	39	---	2
Red pine	3,041	---	---	---	---	2,949	---	---	---	---	88	---	4
White pine	1,104	---	---	---	---	1,094	---	---	---	---	9	---	0
Spruce	1,253	---	---	---	---	1,131	---	---	---	---	25	---	98
Tamarack	437	---	---	---	---	426	---	---	---	---	10	---	0
Softwood total	20,595	---	---	---	---	19,595	---	---	---	---	771	---	229
Hardwoods													
Ash	336	---	---	---	---	251	---	---	---	---	79	---	5
Aspen/balsam poplar	19,302	---	---	---	---	17,246	---	---	---	---	276	---	1,780
Basswood	564	---	---	---	---	547	---	---	---	---	1	---	16
Beech	5,046	---	---	---	---	4,893	---	---	---	---	18	---	135
White birch	2,066	---	---	---	---	1,969	---	4	---	---	64	---	29
Yellow birch	1,086	---	---	---	---	987	---	9	---	---	39	---	51
Black cherry	144	---	---	---	---	126	---	---	---	---	1	---	17
Elm	3	---	---	---	---	3	---	---	---	---	---	---	0
Hard maple	13,860	---	---	---	---	12,400	---	94	---	---	474	---	892
Soft maple	8,249	---	---	---	---	7,859	---	3	---	---	184	---	203
Red oak group	464	---	---	---	---	348	---	0	---	---	100	---	15
Other hardwoods	297	---	---	---	---	294	---	---	---	---	1	---	2
Hardwood total	51,418	---	---	---	---	46,923	---	111	---	---	1,237	---	3,146
State total	72,013	---	---	---	---	66,518	---	111	---	---	2,008	---	3,376

WESTERN UPPER PENINSULA

Species group	Total	Illinois	Indiana	Iowa	Kentucky	Michigan	Minnesota	New York	Pennsylvania	Tennessee	Wisconsin	Other U.S.	Canada
							State of origin						
Softwoods													
Northern white-cedar	35	---	---	---	---	35	---	---	---	---	---	---	---
Balsam fir	2,381	---	---	---	---	1,846	---	---	---	---	535	---	---
Hemlock	1	---	---	---	---	1	---	---	---	---	---	---	---
Jack pine	15,607	---	---	---	---	11,087	---	---	---	---	4,520	---	---
Red pine	8,867	---	---	---	---	5,197	33	---	---	---	3,595	---	42
White pine	389	---	---	---	---	282	---	---	---	---	107	---	---
Spruce	5,403	---	---	---	---	4,038	---	---	---	---	1,356	---	9
Tamarack	650	---	---	---	---	453	---	---	---	---	197	---	---
Softwood total	33,333	---	---	---	---	22,939	33	---	---	---	10,310	---	51
Hardwoods													
Ash	1,541	---	---	---	---	1,080	---	---	---	---	361	---	100
Aspen/balsam poplar	7,678	---	---	---	---	4,974	16	---	---	---	2,572	---	117
Basswood	3,172	---	---	---	---	2,175	---	---	---	---	926	---	70
Beech	2,946	---	---	---	---	1,903	---	---	---	---	769	---	274
White birch	4,201	---	---	---	---	2,821	---	---	---	---	1,092	---	289
Yellow birch	3,131	---	---	---	---	2,343	---	---	---	---	601	---	186
Black cherry	134	---	---	---	---	107	---	---	---	---	12	---	16
Hard maple	27,228	---	---	---	---	19,723	---	---	---	---	5,575	---	1,930
Soft maple	20,854	---	---	---	---	14,100	---	---	---	---	5,042	---	1,712
Red oak group	2,511	---	---	---	---	1,199	---	---	---	---	1,186	---	127
Other hardwoods	16,673	---	---	---	---	11,778	---	---	---	---	4,723	---	172
Hardwood total	90,069	---	---	---	---	62,203	---	---	---	---	22,859	---	4,992
State total	123,403	---	---	---	---	85,142	49	---	---	---	33,169	---	5,042

(Table 4 continued on next page)

(Table 4 continued)

NORTHERN LOWER PENINSULA

Species group	Total	Illinois	Indiana	Iowa	Kentucky	Michigan	Minn-esota	New York	Pennsyl-vania	Tenn-essee	Wisc-onsin	Other U.S.	Canada
Softwoods													
Eastern redcedar	9	--	--	--	--	9	--	--	--	--	--	--	--
Northern white-cedar	1,299	--	--	--	--	1,299	--	--	--	--	--	--	--
Balsam fir	148	--	--	--	--	148	--	--	--	--	--	--	--
Hemlock	256	--	--	--	--	256	--	--	--	--	--	--	--
Jack pine	4,980	--	--	--	--	4,980	--	--	--	--	--	--	--
Red pine	31,468	--	--	--	--	31,468	--	--	--	--	--	--	--
White pine	1,571	--	--	--	--	1,571	--	--	--	--	--	--	--
Other pine	123	--	--	--	--	123	--	--	--	--	--	--	--
Spruce	213	--	--	--	--	213	--	--	--	--	--	--	--
Tamarack	68	--	--	--	--	68	--	--	--	--	--	--	--
Softwood total	40,135	--	--	--	--	40,135	--	--	--	--	--	--	--
Hardwoods													
Ash	3,439	--	--	--	--	3,439	--	--	--	--	--	--	--
Aspen/balsam poplar	30,950	--	--	--	--	30,950	--	--	--	--	--	--	--
Basswood	3,764	--	--	--	--	3,764	--	--	--	--	--	--	--
Beech	871	--	--	--	--	871	--	--	--	--	--	--	--
White birch	1,085	--	--	--	--	1,085	--	--	--	--	--	--	--
Yellow birch	161	--	--	--	--	161	--	--	--	--	--	--	--
Black cherry	901	--	--	--	--	898	--	1	2	--	--	--	--
Black walnut	42	--	--	--	--	42	--	--	--	--	--	--	--
Cottonwood	58	--	--	--	--	58	--	--	--	--	--	--	--
Elm	159	--	--	--	--	159	--	--	--	--	--	--	--
Hickory	153	--	4	--	--	150	--	--	--	--	--	--	--
Hard maple	18,360	--	21	--	--	18,222	--	30	18	--	--	--	70
Soft maple	15,212	--	--	--	--	15,212	--	--	--	--	--	--	--
Red oak group	12,814	--	5	--	--	12,793	--	--	--	--	--	--	16
White oak group	2,713	--	--	--	--	2,713	--	--	--	--	--	--	--
Yellow-poplar	12	--	2	--	--	10	--	--	--	--	--	--	--
Other hardwoods	189	--	--	--	--	189	--	--	--	--	--	--	--
Hardwood total	90,885	--	32	--	--	90,716	--	30	20	--	--	--	86
State total	131,020	--	32	--	--	130,852	--	30	20	--	--	--	86

SOUTHERN LOWER PENINSULA

Species group	Total	Illinois	Indiana	Iowa	Kentucky	Michigan	Minnesota	New York	Pennsylvania	Tennessee	Wisconsin	Other U.S.	Canada
Softwoods													
Eastern redcedar	1	--	--	--	--	1	--	--	--	--	--	--	--
Northern white-cedar	3	--	--	--	--	3	--	--	--	--	--	--	--
Jack pine	3	--	--	--	--	3	--	--	--	--	--	--	--
Loblolly/shortleaf pine	32	--	--	--	--	--	--	--	--	--	--	32	--
Red pine	163	--	--	--	--	163	--	--	--	--	--	0	--
White pine	133	--	--	--	--	133	--	--	--	--	--	--	--
Other pine	179	--	--	--	--	179	--	--	--	--	--	--	--
Softwood total	514	--	--	--	--	482	--	--	--	--	--	33	--
Hardwoods													
Ash	1,664	--	0	--	--	1,663	--	--	--	--	--	1	--
Aspen/balsam poplar	768	--	--	--	--	768	--	--	--	--	--	--	--
Basswood	289	--	0	--	--	288	--	--	--	--	--	--	--
Beech	157	--	--	--	--	157	--	--	--	--	--	--	--
White birch	37	--	--	--	--	37	--	--	--	--	--	--	--
Yellow birch	10	--	--	--	--	10	--	--	--	--	--	--	--
Black cherry	1,953	--	3	--	--	1,888	--	--	61	--	--	1	--
Black walnut	660	18	21	--	18	560	--	--	--	21	--	1	--
Cottonwood	235	--	--	--	--	234	--	--	--	--	--	0	--
Elm	219	--	0	--	--	219	--	--	--	--	--	--	--
Hickory	317	2	4	--	5	303	--	--	--	2	--	0	--
Hard maple	4,415	--	11	--	--	4,400	--	--	--	--	--	4	--
Soft maple	3,984	--	3	--	--	3,980	--	--	--	--	--	1	--
Red oak group	4,649	--	2	--	--	4,495	--	--	151	--	--	0	--
White oak group	1,731	50	50	--	83	1,431	--	--	--	58	--	1	--
Sycamore	117	--	--	--	--	117	--	--	--	--	--	--	--
Yellow-poplar	75	--	4	--	--	71	--	--	--	--	--	--	--
Other hardwoods	271	--	--	--	--	271	--	--	--	--	--	--	--
Hardwood total	21,550	70	100	--	102	20,893	--	--	212	81	--	10	--
State total	22,065	70	100	--	102	21,374	--	--	212	81	--	43	--

All table cells without observations are indicated by --. Table value of 0 indicates the volume rounds to less than 1 thousand cubic feet. Columns and rows may not add to their totals due to rounding.

Table 5.--Industrial roundwood production by mill type, hardwoods and softwoods, and survey year, Michigan

(In thousand cubic feet)

ALL SPECIES

Kind of mill	\ Survey Year \ 1990	1992	1994	1996	1998	2000	2004	2006
Saw mills	110,420.7	108,866.4	113,313.6	98,486.6	130,933.9	130,634.3	121,549.3	127,670.5
Veneer mills	7,025.0	6,226.3	8,001.1	9,857.5	6,672.7	8,198.7	6,039.2	5,410.7
Pulp and composite product mills	214,630.6	209,274.1	238,012.4	223,885.9	210,261.5	211,435.6	209,985.9	162,927.0
Cabin log mills	1,316.2	1,002.4	711.6	1,173.5	1,603.1	1,858.4	1,647.6	562.2
Industrial fuelwood[a]	15,445.1	18,029.6	23,781.2	19,372.3	18,107.3	8,869.8	10,088.3	27,359.0
Post and poles	2,684.2	2,986.3	2,372.7	2,749.3	2,337.2	3,689.9	4,143.9	5,459.9
Other products[b]	1,046.0	378.2	719.4	557.0	593.3	732.1	691.9	507.4
Total	352,567.8	346,763.3	386,912.0	356,082.1	370,509.0	365,418.8	354,146.1	329,896.7

SOFTWOODS

Kind of mill	1990	1992	1994	1996	1998	2000	2004	2006
Saw mills	23,969.0	24,100.4	24,614.4	23,239.7	36,207.3	42,146.1	45,127.4	52,022.0
Veneer mills	644.9	196.3	201.0	502.1	431.9	398.4	329.7	417.8
Pulp and composite product mills	41,279.4	44,739.7	46,786.5	47,495.3	40,154.1	38,538.7	39,805.5	24,334.7
Cabin log mills	1,316.2	1,002.4	711.6	1,173.5	1,580.0	1,858.4	1,647.6	556.2
Industrial fuelwood[a]	2,976.1	8,655.8	7,776.9	12,621.9	6,649.1	2,553.8	2,284.3	6,473.3
Post and poles	2,684.2	2,986.3	2,352.7	2,129.3	2,314.8	3,689.9	4,143.9	5,459.9
Other products[b]	16.0	47.8	20.1	13.4	16.9	3.6	2.1	41.4
Total	72,885.8	81,728.7	82,463.2	87,175.2	87,354.1	89,188.9	93,340.5	89,305.3

HARDWOODS

Kind of mill	1990	1992	1994	1996	1998	2000	2004	2006
Saw mills	86,451.7	84,766.0	88,699.1	75,247.0	94,726.7	88,488.3	76,421.9	75,648.5
Veneer mills	6,380.1	6,030.0	7,800.2	9,355.4	6,240.9	7,800.2	5,709.5	4,992.9
Pulp and composite product mills	173,351.2	164,534.4	191,225.9	176,390.7	170,107.4	172,896.9	170,180.3	138,592.3
Cabin log mills	--	--	--	--	23.0	--	--	6.0
Industrial fuelwood[a]	12,469.0	9,373.8	16,004.3	6,750.3	11,458.1	6,316.0	7,804.1	20,885.6
Post and poles	--	--	20.0	620.0	22.4	--	--	--
Other products[b]	1,030.0	330.3	699.2	543.6	576.4	728.5	689.8	466.0
Total	279,682.0	265,034.5	304,448.7	268,907.0	283,154.9	276,229.9	260,805.6	240,591.3

[a] Does not include residential fuelwood.
[b] Includes plants producing mulch, mine timbers, excelsior, shavings, etc.
All table cells without observations are indicated by --. Table value of 0.0 indicates the volume rounds to less than 0.1 thousand cubic feet. Columns and rows may not add to their totals due to rounding.

Table 6. -- Industrial roundwood production by Forest Inventory Unit, species group, and State of destination, Michigan, 2006

(In thousand cubic feet)

ALL UNITS

Species group	Total	State of destination								Other countries
		Indiana	Kentucky	Michigan	Minnesota	Ohio	Virginia	Wisconsin	Canada	
Softwoods										
Eastern redcedar	10	--	--	10	--	--	--	--	--	--
Northern white-cedar	4,673	--	--	4,602	2	--	--	69	--	--
Balsam fir	6,070	--	--	5,029	49	--	--	271	720	--
Hemlock	4,654	--	--	4,478	--	--	--	176	--	--
Jack pine	20,672	--	--	19,543	1	--	--	326	801	1
Red pine	40,462	2	--	39,777	1	--	--	567	116	--
White pine	3,391	14	--	3,080	0	--	--	127	169	1
Other pine	302	--	--	302	--	--	--	--	--	--
Spruce	8,065	--	--	5,382	2	--	--	1,710	970	--
Tamarack	1,007	--	--	947	--	--	--	60	--	--
Softwood total	89,305	16	--	83,151	56	--	--	3,306	2,777	--
Hardwoods										
Ash	7,175	314	3	6,433	129	16	1	265	15	--
Aspen/balsam poplar	57,371	--	--	53,938	367	--	--	2,761	305	10
Basswood	7,354	70	--	6,774	--	--	--	498	3	--
Beech	8,207	16	--	7,825	10	1	--	343	13	--
White birch	6,585	0	--	5,913	58	--	--	307	306	1
Yellow birch	4,070	--	--	3,501	--	--	--	478	90	1
Other birch	4	--	--	4	--	--	--	4	--	--
Black cherry	3,491	390	--	3,019	--	3	1	76	2	0
Black walnut	792	174	3	601	--	8	--	2	3	0
Cottonwood	365	68	--	292	--	1	--	4	--	--
Elm	426	16	--	381	--	--	--	25	3	--
Hickory	575	109	--	453	--	--	1	13	1	--
Hard maple	59,887	457	2	54,745	771	250	1	3,547	112	--
Soft maple	45,637	330	--	41,152	2,612	3	--	1,539	1	--
Red oak group	20,805	728	9	18,835	--	112	--	958	157	6
White oak group	4,762	453	0	4,144	--	42	1	29	92	--
Sycamore	138	20	--	117	--	1	--	--	--	--
Yellow-poplar	253	169	--	81	--	2	--	--	--	--
Other Hardwoods	12,693	12	--	12,532	--	--	--	145	2	--
Hardwood total	240,591	3,328	17	220,735	3,948	441	5	10,993	1,106	19
State total	329,897	3,344	17	303,886	4,004	441	5	14,299	3,883	19

(Table 6 continued on next page)

(Table 6 continued)

EASTERN UPPER PENINSULA

Species group	Total		State of destiniation							Other countries
		Indiana	Kentucky	Michigan	Minnesota	Ohio	Virginia	Wisconsin	Canada	
Softwoods										
Northern white-cedar	3,045	--	--	2,977	--	--	--	69	--	--
Balsam fir	2,676	--	--	2,081	49	--	--	94	452	--
Hemlock	1,576	--	--	1,487	--	--	--	90	--	--
Jack pine	8,259	--	--	8,011	0	--	--	110	137	--
Red pine	5,110	--	--	4,587	0	--	--	406	116	--
White pine	631	--	--	495	--	--	--	32	104	--
Spruce	3,380	--	--	2,294	0	--	--	462	624	--
Tamarack	335	--	--	311	--	--	--	24	--	--
Softwood total	25,013	--	--	22,244	49	--	--	1,286	1,434	--
Hardwoods										
Ash	515	--	0	503	7	--	--	5	--	--
Aspen/balsam poplar	11,032	--	--	10,312	20	--	--	538	162	--
Basswood	798	--	--	793	--	--	--	3	0	3
Beech	3,709	--	--	3,378	1	--	--	329	1	--
White birch	2,349	--	--	2,053	3	--	--	20	272	1
Yellow birch	1,325	--	--	1,186	--	--	--	49	90	--
Black cherry	140	--	--	128	--	--	0	11	--	0
Elm	3	--	--	2	--	--	--	1	--	--
Hickory	0	--	--	--	--	--	--	0	--	--
Hard maple	14,552	--	0	13,670	43	--	0	751	89	--
Soft maple	11,337	--	--	10,431	144	--	--	762	0	--
Red oak group	644	--	--	586	--	--	--	56	--	2
White oak group	6	--	--	5	--	--	--	1	--	--
Other hardwoods	1,749	--	--	1,749	--	--	--	--	--	--
Hardwood total	48,161	--	1	44,797	218	--	1	2,525	614	6
State total	73,173	--	1	67,041	266	--	1	3,811	2,048	6

WESTERN UPPER PENINSULA

		State of destiniation								
Species group	Total	Indiana	Kentucky	Michigan	Minnesota	Ohio	Virginia	Wisconsin	Canada	Other countries
Softwoods										
Northern white-cedar	772	--	--	772	--	--	--	0	--	--
Balsam fir	2,979	--	--	2,774	1	--	--	174	30	--
Hemlock	2,799	--	--	2,716	--	--	--	82	--	--
Jack pine	4,920	--	--	4,826	1	--	--	93	--	--
Red pine	3,779	--	--	3,629	1	--	--	150	--	--
White pine	1,000	--	--	906	0	--	--	95	--	--
Spruce	4,169	--	--	2,878	2	--	--	1,243	46	--
Tamarack	602	--	--	566	--	--	--	36	--	--
Softwood total	21,021	--	--	19,067	5	--	--	1,873	76	--
Hardwoods										
Ash	1,210	--	1	828	122	--	0	260	--	--
Aspen/balsam poplar	13,038	--	--	10,467	347	--	--	2,223	--	--
Basswood	2,388	--	--	1,885	--	--	--	495	--	8
Beech	3,416	--	--	3,393	9	--	--	14	--	--
White birch	3,065	--	--	2,722	55	--	--	287	--	1
Yellow birch	2,563	--	--	2,133	--	--	--	429	--	1
River birch	4	--	--	--	--	--	--	4	--	--
Black cherry	197	--	--	132	--	--	0	64	--	0
Black walnut	2	--	--	--	--	--	--	2	--	--
Cottonwood	4	--	--	--	--	--	--	4	--	--
Elm	26	--	--	2	--	--	--	24	--	--
Hickory	13	--	--	--	--	--	--	13	--	--
Hard maple	22,387	--	2	18,860	729	--	1	2,795	--	--
Soft maple	14,888	--	--	11,643	2,468	--	--	777	--	--
Red oak group	1,921	--	--	1,017	--	--	--	900	--	4
White oak group	33	--	--	5	--	--	--	28	--	--
Other hardwoods	10,459	--	--	10,314	--	--	--	145	--	--
Hardwood total	75,613	--	3	63,401	3,730	--	1	8,464	--	14
State total	96,634	--	3	82,467	3,735	--	1	10,338	76	14

(Table 6 continued on next page)

31

(Table 6 continued)

NORTHERN LOWER PENINSULA

Species group	Total	Indiana	Kentucky	Michigan	Minnesota	Ohio	Virginia	Wisconsin	Canada	Other countries
Softwoods										
Eastern redcedar	9	--	--	9	--	--	--	--	--	--
Northern white-cedar	855	--	--	853	2	--	--	--	--	--
Balsam fir	405	--	--	164	--	--	--	3	238	--
Hemlock	269	--	--	265	--	--	--	4	--	--
Jack pine	7,329	--	--	6,542	--	--	--	123	663	--
Red pine	29,572	--	--	29,561	--	--	--	11	--	--
White pine	1,588	--	--	1,522	--	--	--	--	65	--
Other pine	113	--	--	113	--	--	--	--	--	--
Spruce	513	--	--	208	--	--	--	5	300	--
Tamarack	69	--	--	68	--	--	--	1	--	--
Softwood total	40,723	--	--	39,308	2	--	--	146	1,267	--
Hardwoods										
Ash	3,400	--	0	3,389	--	--	1	--	9	--
Aspen/balsam poplar	32,451	--	--	32,309	--	--	--	--	143	--
Basswood	3,826	--	--	3,824	--	--	--	--	2	--
Beech	908	--	--	908	--	--	--	--	0	--
White birch	1,154	--	--	1,120	--	--	--	--	34	--
Yellow birch	166	--	--	165	--	--	--	--	1	--
Black cherry	867	--	--	866	--	--	0	--	1	0
Black walnut	5	--	--	5	--	--	--	--	--	--
Cottonwood	102	--	--	102	--	--	--	--	--	--
Elm	146	--	--	145	--	--	--	--	0	--
Hickory	34	--	--	34	--	--	--	--	--	--
Hard maple	20,325	--	0	20,308	--	--	--	0	17	--
Soft maple	15,081	--	--	15,079	--	--	--	0	1	--
Red oak group	12,970	--	6	12,828	--	--	--	0	136	--
White oak group	2,695	--	0	2,655	--	--	0	--	39	--
Yellow-poplar	2	--	--	2	--	--	--	--	--	--
Other hardwoods	196	--	--	196	--	--	--	--	1	--
Hardwood total	94,329	--	7	93,936	--	--	1	1	384	0
State total	135,051	--	7	133,244	2	--	1	147	1,650	0

SOUTHERN LOWER PENINSULA

Species group	Total	Indiana	Kentucky	Michigan	Minnesota	Ohio	Virginia	Wisconsin	Canada	Other countries
Softwoods										
Eastern redcedar	1	--	--	1	--	--	--	--	--	--
Northern white-cedar	0	--	--	0	--	--	--	--	--	--
Balsam fir	9	--	--	9	--	--	--	--	--	--
Hemlock	10	--	--	10	--	--	--	--	--	--
Jack pine	164	--	--	164	--	--	--	--	--	--
Red pine	2,001	2	--	1,999	--	--	--	--	--	--
White pine	171	14	--	157	--	--	--	--	--	--
Other pine	189	--	--	189	--	--	--	--	--	--
Spruce	2	--	--	2	--	--	--	--	--	--
Tamarack	1	--	--	1	--	--	--	--	--	--
Softwood total	2,549	16	--	2,533	--	--	--	--	--	--
Hardwoods										
Ash	2,050	314	1	1,713	--	16	0	--	6	--
Aspen/balsam poplar	849	--	--	849	--	--	--	--	--	--
Basswood	342	70	--	271	--	--	--	--	1	--
Beech	174	16	--	145	--	1	--	--	12	--
White birch	17	0	--	17	--	--	--	--	--	--
Yellow birch	16	--	--	16	--	--	--	--	--	--
Black cherry	2,287	390	--	1,892	--	3	--	--	1	--
Black walnut	784	174	3	596	--	8	--	--	3	0
Cottonwood	260	68	--	190	--	1	--	--	2	--
Elm	252	16	--	233	--	--	--	--	--	--
Hickory	529	109	--	419	--	--	1	--	1	--
Hard maple	2,623	457	--	1,908	--	250	--	1	7	--
Soft maple	4,332	330	--	3,998	--	3	--	1	--	--
Red oak group	5,269	728	2	4,404	--	112	--	1	21	--
White oak group	2,028	453	0	1,479	--	42	1	--	53	--
Sycamore	138	20	--	117	--	1	--	--	--	--
Yellow-poplar	251	169	--	79	--	2	--	--	--	--
Other hardwoods	288	12	--	274	--	--	--	--	2	--
Hardwood total	22,489	3,328	6	18,601	--	441	2	3	108	0
State total	25,038	3,344	6	21,134	--	441	2	3	108	0

All table cells without observations are indicated by -- . Table value of 0 indicates the volume rounds to less than 1 thousand cubic feet. Columns and rows may not add to their totals due to rounding.

Table 7.-- Industrial roundwood production by Forest Inventory Unit, county, and species group, Michigan, 2006

(In thousand cubic feet)

Forest Inventory Unit and county	All species	Softwoods											Hardwoods			
		Eastern red-cedar	Northern white-cedar	Balsam fir	Hemlock	Jack pine	Red pine	White pine	Other pine	Spruce	Tama-rack	Total softwoods	Ash	Aspen/balsam poplar	Bass-wood	Beech
Eastern Upper Peninsula																
Alger	12,486	--	66	312	334	492	1,037	266	--	301	42	2,849	85	3,357	84	667
Chippewa	9,016	--	166	388	187	2,548	758	55	--	845	11	4,959	50	838	32	277
Delta	12,018	--	815	450	256	979	886	82	--	404	59	3,931	104	1,407	149	639
Luce	12,147	--	151	386	222	2,006	452	62	--	692	36	4,007	87	1,162	64	845
Mackinac	7,810	--	150	272	60	461	851	52	--	436	18	2,300	55	1,729	91	306
Menominee	10,503	--	1,546	614	403	274	313	75	--	412	138	3,774	62	1,356	274	448
Schoolcraft	9,193	--	151	255	115	1,499	812	41	--	289	31	3,193	72	1,184	106	527
Total	73,173	--	3,045	2,676	1,576	8,259	5,110	631	--	3,380	335	25,013	515	11,032	798	3,709
Western Upper Peninsula																
Baraga	12,730	--	44	302	493	452	308	49	--	361	41	2,050	134	1,835	253	778
Dickinson	9,781	--	183	436	105	337	349	105	--	601	120	2,236	77	1,386	461	286
Gogebic	9,479	--	26	136	122	17	396	50	--	321	15	1,084	258	991	249	136
Houghton	10,859	--	63	170	337	667	516	11	--	255	27	2,047	165	1,408	302	246
Iron	13,413	--	67	690	209	520	728	93	--	1,085	166	3,559	132	1,574	404	239
Keweenaw	5,060	--	33	84	59	20	40	5	--	112	8	361	107	221	112	180
Marquette	24,870	--	187	949	1,102	2,761	1,100	621	--	1,077	194	7,992	115	3,580	265	1,322
Ontonagon	10,441	--	168	211	371	147	341	67	--	357	30	1,692	223	2,042	342	229
Total	96,634	--	772	2,979	2,799	4,920	3,779	1,000	--	4,169	602	21,021	1,210	13,038	2,388	3,416
Northern Lower Peninsula																
Alcona	5,727	--	75	7	4	181	715	47	0	18	3	1,049	214	2,641	61	18
Alpena	3,753	7	232	37	18	60	426	47	2	61	5	894	157	1,584	78	18
Antrim	4,279	--	7	0	--	33	439	1	2	0	--	482	177	596	489	59
Arenac	1,028	0	2	0	--	109	39	22	--	0	--	175	63	306	11	6
Bay	317	--	--	--	2	2	--	2	--	--	--	6	20	115	14	--
Benzie	3,407	--	--	--	14	55	598	9	--	0	--	675	99	404	88	35
Charlevoix	2,784	--	39	9	7	1	314	30	6	8	7	416	123	493	346	36
Cheboygan	5,636	--	62	54	7	363	983	89	0	79	11	1,648	110	1,887	275	41
Clare	5,995	--	12	2	6	283	910	15	--	0	2	1,230	101	2,563	26	37
Crawford	6,209	--	8	2	2	1,177	1,672	48	1	13	1	2,924	15	1,365	73	12
Emmet	3,471	--	18	11	3	34	300	22	8	11	5	413	203	668	269	24
Gladwin	3,021	--	2	0	1	76	337	17	--	0	0	433	74	1,345	33	22
Grand Traverse	4,239	--	14	2	9	90	1,581	100	6	3	7	1,812	86	307	106	17
Iosco	4,586	1	22	12	7	598	2,128	65	--	8	4	2,845	62	634	20	8
Isabella	1,987	--	12	2	3	8	139	3	6	--	2	162	128	762	62	4
Kalkaska	7,024	--	11	8	8	407	2,567	84	9	3	2	3,100	86	968	283	49
Lake	5,595	--	12	--	8	606	1,697	91	1	3	2	2,420	47	574	49	36
Leelanau	2,166	--	--	1	29	18	186	41	1	0	4	279	154	113	84	24
Manistee	6,878	--	--	0	12	163	1,731	93	2	--	1	2,001	163	1,145	83	104
Mason	3,817	--	3	0	16	116	1,008	37	4	1	--	1,184	53	781	26	27
Mecosta	3,017	--	--	0	0	23	417	110	25	7	1	610	90	1,057	27	26
Midland	1,444	--	--	--	26	6	15	78	1	--	--	99	125	432	25	2
Missaukee	4,486	--	13	5	10	177	1,132	30	3	7	6	1,383	94	1,310	143	14
Montmorency	4,877	--	18	82	3	326	596	116	1	83	2	1,228	61	1,769	234	30
Newaygo	4,365	--	--	--	14	252	749	70	12	--	--	1,096	119	371	49	17
Oceana	2,487	--	--	--	17	71	768	13	7	1	--	876	100	172	27	22

County																
Ogemaw	3,665	0	15	5	4	231	597	44	--	2	--	898	1,422	114	31	13
Osceola	2,834	--	9	1	21	31	719	30	11	--	0	822	643	108	36	12
Oscoda	5,421	--	8	18	--	847	1,262	55	2	21	1	2,211	1,599	41	41	44
Otsego	4,853	--	4	32	2	287	1,186	59	--	37	1	1,610	833	50	452	37
Presque Isle	3,939	--	220	105	3	278	463	30	--	135	2	1,237	1,415	77	116	31
Roscommon	3,647	--	34	10	1	226	735	50	0	2	1	1,059	979	81	7	6
Wexford	8,099	--	17	2	9	196	3,163	38	10	8	1	3,444	1,199	204	162	78
Total	135,051	9	855	405	269	7,329	29,572	1,588	113	513	69	40,723	32,451	3,400	3,826	908
Southern Lower Peninsula																
Allegan	1,730	--	--	--	--	--	72	29	117	--	--	218	--	98	6	9
Barry	1,508	--	--	--	--	29	50	--	--	--	--	79	4	18	16	7
Berrien	504	--	--	--	--	--	--	--	--	--	--	--	--	14	4	3
Branch	533	--	--	--	--	--	--	--	--	--	--	--	--	47	5	4
Calhoun	947	--	--	--	--	--	--	--	58	--	--	58	--	97	27	5
Cass	432	--	--	--	--	--	4	7	--	--	--	11	--	12	4	2
Clinton	360	--	0	9	10	45	13	1	--	2	1	82	2	30	6	0
Eaton	706	--	--	--	--	--	142	1	--	--	--	142	1	95	20	17
Genesee	440	--	--	--	--	--	--	1	--	--	--	1	7	66	9	2
Gratiot	441	--	--	--	--	--	8	4	--	--	--	11	60	91	15	7
Hillsdale	379	--	--	--	--	--	--	--	--	--	--	--	0	16	5	3
Huron	285	--	--	--	--	--	0	--	--	--	--	0	75	45	1	--
Ingham	304	--	--	--	--	--	--	--	--	--	--	--	--	74	11	2
Ionia	670	--	--	--	--	--	30	0	1	31	--	31	2	40	18	31
Jackson	939	--	--	--	--	--	--	--	--	--	--	--	3	43	14	2
Kalamazoo	858	--	--	--	--	--	57	1	--	--	--	59	4	51	4	3
Kent	2,585	--	--	--	--	14	91	3	1	--	--	109	16	226	37	4
Lapeer	499	--	--	--	--	--	1	--	--	1	--	1	9	53	6	1
Lenawee	309	--	--	--	--	--	--	4	--	--	--	--	--	20	16	4
Livingston	676	--	--	--	--	--	--	0	0	0	--	0	1	59	1	0
Macomb	354	--	--	--	--	--	37	--	--	37	--	37	18	62	3	1
Monroe	134	--	--	--	--	--	--	--	--	--	--	0	--	40	1	0
Montcalm	1,585	--	--	--	--	44	140	50	1	--	--	234	174	130	18	8
Muskegon	2,099	--	--	--	--	28	672	60	6	--	--	766	100	26	4	17
Oakland	489	--	--	--	--	--	--	0	--	--	--	0	--	52	6	1
Ottawa	1,095	--	--	--	--	4	575	0	4	--	--	579	21	60	2	8
Saginaw	567	--	--	--	--	--	1	5	--	--	--	10	15	86	17	2
Sanilac	370	--	--	--	--	1	3	1	--	--	--	5	115	84	8	1
Shiawassee	171	--	--	--	--	--	1	--	--	--	--	1	0	38	8	1
St. Clair	513	1	--	--	--	--	2	2	--	--	--	4	5	96	20	1
St. Joseph	554	--	--	--	--	--	1	7	--	--	--	8	0	38	7	3
Tuscola	516	--	--	--	--	--	--	--	--	--	--	--	218	56	9	0
Van Buren	713	--	--	--	--	--	105	--	--	--	--	105	--	38	5	16
Washtenaw	455	--	--	--	--	--	--	0	--	--	--	0	1	20	4	--
Wayne	320	--	--	--	--	--	--	8	0	--	--	0	--	27	7	8
Total	25,038	1	0	9	10	164	2,001	171	189	2	1	2,549	849	2,050	342	174
State total	329,897	10	4,673	6,070	4,654	20,672	40,462	3,391	302	8,065	1,007	89,305	57,371	7,175	7,354	8,207

(Table 7 continued on the next page)

(Table 7 continued)

	Hardwoods															
Forest Inventory Unit and county	White birch	Yellow birch	Other birch	Black cherry	Black walnut	Cotton-wood	Elm	Hickory	Hard maple	Soft maple	Red oak group	White oak group	Syca-more	Yellow-poplar	Other hardwoods	Total hardwoods
Eastern Upper Peninsula																
Alger	443	281	--	53	--	--	0	--	2,634	1,727	69	5	--	--	231	9,637
Chippewa	212	117	--	2	--	--	0	--	1,418	963	103	--	--	--	45	4,057
Delta	496	257	--	42	--	--	0	--	2,555	2,056	73	--	--	--	308	8,087
Luce	314	198	--	12	--	--	1	--	2,788	2,496	86	--	--	--	86	8,141
Mackinac	267	124	--	5	--	--	0	--	1,709	1,103	67	--	--	--	54	5,510
Menominee	279	158	--	11	--	--	1	0	1,648	1,442	185	1	--	--	865	6,729
Schoolcraft	338	189	--	15	--	--	0	--	1,799	1,550	61	--	--	--	160	6,000
Total	2,349	1,325	--	140	--	--	3	0	14,552	11,337	644	6	--	--	1,749	48,161
Western Upper Peninsula																
Baraga	467	425	--	13	--	--	1	--	3,553	2,351	139	3	--	--	728	10,680
Dickinson	292	185	2	6	--	0	1	0	1,628	1,197	103	0	--	--	1,921	7,545
Gogebic	298	308	2	49	0	3	21	9	2,733	2,714	284	8	--	--	333	8,395
Houghton	326	352	--	8	1	--	0	--	3,397	1,342	363	3	--	--	897	8,812
Iron	316	314	1	37	1	--	1	0	2,594	1,277	154	3	--	--	2,808	9,854
Keweenaw	269	236	--	8	0	--	--	2	1,663	1,410	296	3	--	--	191	4,699
Marquette	774	473	--	56	1	--	1	--	4,520	3,046	383	11	--	--	2,330	16,877
Ontonagon	322	270	--	20	--	0	2	0	2,298	1,549	199	2	--	--	1,251	8,749
Total	3,065	2,563	4	197	2	4	26	13	22,387	14,888	1,921	33	--	--	10,459	75,613
Northern Lower Peninsula																
Alcona	72	2	--	7	--	--	1	--	141	516	967	38	--	--	--	4,678
Alpena	70	6	--	0	--	1	2	--	131	465	326	20	--	0	--	2,859
Antrim	56	4	--	34	--	--	2	--	2,004	331	41	--	--	--	5	3,796
Arenac	16	1	--	1	--	12	5	0	22	264	122	26	--	--	--	853
Bay	3	--	--	0	--	2	2	0	1	123	6	26	--	--	--	311
Benzie	13	8	--	79	--	--	2	--	1,493	428	72	--	--	--	10	2,732
Charlevoix	57	17	--	5	--	--	2	--	1,105	132	43	6	--	--	1	2,368
Cheboygan	143	18	--	0	--	--	3	--	687	691	116	11	--	--	5	3,987
Clare	19	--	--	20	--	3	11	4	427	798	596	143	--	--	18	4,765
Crawford	40	0	--	10	--	--	0	--	410	783	493	84	--	--	--	3,284
Emmet	31	7	--	20	--	--	2	0	1,504	270	54	4	--	--	2	3,058
Gladwin	14	--	--	7	--	15	4	1	177	637	183	66	--	--	11	2,588
Grand Traverse	8	6	--	20	--	--	4	--	1,107	293	335	134	--	--	4	2,427
Iosco	48	0	--	2	--	38	1	0	57	573	267	31	--	--	--	1,741
Isabella	7	--	--	24	0	8	10	7	213	354	176	69	--	0	1	1,826
Kalkaska	94	3	--	60	--	--	1	0	1,488	678	205	9	--	--	0	3,924
Lake	5	--	--	27	--	1	1	--	303	345	1,436	337	--	--	15	3,175
Leelanau	17	1	--	26	0	--	11	--	1,108	186	162	2	--	0	--	1,887
Manistee	15	1	--	105	--	--	3	1	1,345	784	867	216	--	0	44	4,876
Mason	7	3	--	25	--	0	6	--	283	470	682	261	--	--	8	2,633
Mecosta	10	2	--	39	1	--	12	6	443	318	306	61	--	0	--	2,408
Midland	11	--	--	7	1	8	5	5	50	433	88	154	--	0	10	1,345
Missaukee	23	4	--	25	0	--	4	--	598	588	246	48	--	--	0	3,103
Montmorency	77	0	--	4	--	--	0	--	389	536	507	42	--	--	5	3,649
Newaygo	8	5	--	75	--	0	10	4	353	515	1,321	421	--	1	--	3,269
Oceana	2	9	--	68	2	3	8	2	316	348	401	128	--	--	1	1,610

County																Total
Ogemaw	28	3	--	3	--	11	4	--	--	190	476	421	48	--	4	2,768
Osceola	14	43	--	30	--	--	7	4	--	462	255	377	19	--	1	2,011
Oscoda	20	3	--	8	--	0	0	--	--	253	531	624	37	--	7	3,209
Otsego	57	7	--	11	--	--	3	--	--	1,273	398	99	16	--	6	3,242
Presque Isle	137	4	--	0	--	--	3	--	--	257	527	127	7	--	--	2,702
Roscommon	25	2	--	3	--	--	3	--	--	--	523	742	164	--	2	2,588
Wexford	9	6	--	124	--	--	15	0	--	49	512	561	66	--	33	4,655
Total	1,154	166	--	867	5	102	146	34	1,685	20,325	15,081	12,970	2,695	2	196	94,329
Southern Lower Peninsula																
Allegan	1	1	--	136	46	0	1	20	49	249	301	216	117	116	147	1,513
Barry	--	0	--	174	75	0	1	30	286	202	360	133	0	4	118	1,430
Berrien	0	--	--	118	5	4	4	8	156	45	54	18	15	57	1	504
Branch	--	--	--	85	57	6	2	11	57	98	95	55	1	9	1	533
Calhoun	--	--	--	222	25	4	2	39	49	206	184	24	1	2	1	889
Cass	--	0	--	177	44	0	5	18	32	43	65	13	--	6	1	421
Clinton	--	--	--	12	19	8	3	10	29	109	41	8	0	0	--	278
Eaton	--	--	--	43	21	2	5	25	136	121	51	23	3	3	0	565
Genesee	0	0	--	13	3	4	3	10	62	99	96	66	--	--	--	439
Gratiot	0	--	--	10	1	5	4	4	66	56	76	31	--	1	1	429
Hillsdale	--	--	--	63	49	1	2	10	89	24	71	44	1	1	1	379
Huron	0	0	--	3	--	33	0	0	8	56	56	5	--	--	--	285
Ingham	--	--	--	34	58	11	8	6	30	38	19	12	0	0	--	304
Ionia	--	--	--	54	77	3	2	24	103	133	105	45	--	2	2	640
Jackson	--	--	--	182	30	7	4	87	19	65	359	120	1	3	2	939
Kalamazoo	--	--	--	219	18	2	2	11	72	116	233	65	1	1	--	799
Kent	7	10	--	160	9	1	26	42	470	547	738	180	--	3	0	2,476
Lapeer	0	0	--	20	1	8	9	9	89	105	106	90	--	--	3	498
Lenawee	--	--	--	25	13	2	0	21	103	24	46	33	0	2	--	309
Livingston	--	--	--	78	1	1	117	4	9	181	170	52	--	0	0	675
Macomb	--	1	--	4	0	2	3	2	5	207	6	5	--	0	--	317
Monroe	--	--	--	3	12	4	0	9	9	40	13	4	0	0	0	134
Montcalm	5	0	--	37	3	0	8	8	99	285	395	178	--	1	1	1,350
Muskegon	0	2	--	20	3	--	3	3	92	285	646	130	--	1	3	1,333
Oakland	--	--	--	55	1	2	2	13	30	109	142	76	0	--	0	489
Ottawa	--	1	--	57	13	1	1	1	109	77	147	17	0	1	1	516
Saginaw	1	--	--	8	2	2	2	12	20	192	97	93	--	1	--	557
Sanilac	0	--	--	7	--	10	18	0	31	80	4	2	--	--	--	366
Shiawassee	--	--	--	10	3	15	1	5	12	50	25	12	--	--	--	170
St. Clair	0	1	--	6	0	2	5	5	14	144	40	93	0	--	4	509
St. Joseph	--	0	--	93	69	62	17	33	31	76	158	19	1	1	2	546
Tuscola	3	0	--	9	1	4	1	1	59	102	24	13	--	10	--	516
Van Buren	--	--	--	127	58	18	2	23	123	47	133	16	0	17	1	608
Washtenaw	--	0	--	22	79	1	2	24	23	44	116	118	--	--	--	455
Wayne	--	--	--	4	0	23	1	2	52	74	95	17	0	7	3	320
Total	17	16	--	2,287	784	260	252	529	2,623	4,332	5,269	2,028	138	251	288	22,489
State total	6,585	4,070	16	3,491	792	365	426	575	59,887	45,637	20,805	4,762	138	253	12,693	240,591

All table cells without observations are indicated by --. Table value of 0 indicates the volume rounds to less than 1 thousand cubic feet. Columns and rows may not add to their totals due to rounding.

Table 8.-- Industrial roundwood production by Forest Inventory Unit, species group, and product, Michigan, 2006

ALL UNITS

Species group	All products MCF[a]	Saw logs MBF[b]	Saw logs MCF[a]	Veneer logs MBF[b]	Veneer logs MCF[a]	Pulp and composite products Cords[c]	Pulp and composite products MCF[a]	Cabin logs MCF[a]	Excelsior/ shaving/ mulch MCF[c]	Industrial fuelwood Cords[c]	Industrial fuelwood MCF[a]	Poles Pieces	Poles MCF[a]	Posts[d] M pieces	Posts[d] MCF[a]	Miscel-laneous MCF[a]
Softwoods																
Eastern redcedar	10	10	2	--	--	--	--	1	--	--	--	--	--	7	7	--
Northern white-cedar	4,673	6,205	1,168	--	--	1,290	102	231	--	--	--	--	--	3,084	3,170	2
Balsam fir	6,070	6,610	1,245	--	--	58,154	4,594	--	--	2,089	146	--	--	82	85	--
Hemlock	4,654	342	57	--	--	55,196	4,361	--	--	3,377	236	--	--	--	--	--
Jack pine	20,672	73,030	13,752	--	--	79,460	6,277	--	3	9,147	639	--	--	--	--	--
Red pine	40,462	180,790	30,318	1,015	165	45,362	3,584	199	21	56,931	3,979	98,605	592	1,560	1,604	--
White pine	3,391	9,391	1,575	669	109	7,547	596	124	11	13,922	973	--	--	3	3	--
Other pine	302	192	36	--	--	--	--	--	4	3,747	262	--	--	--	--	--
Spruce	8,065	20,545	3,869	883	144	49,130	3,881	2	--	2,428	170	--	--	--	--	--
Tamarack	1,007	--	--	--	--	11,894	940	--	--	968	68	--	--	--	--	--
Softwood total	89,305	297,115	52,022	2,567	418	308,034	24,335	556	40	92,608	6,473	98,605	592	4,736	4,868	2
Hardwoods																
Ash	7,175	20,094	3,384	367	60	24,105	1,904	1	46	25,467	1,780	--	--	--	--	
Aspen/balsam poplar	57,371	52,331	9,205	9,138	1,488	559,155	44,173	--	27	35,450	2,478	--	--	--	--	
Basswood	7,354	16,417	2,883	131	21	45,926	3,628	--	10	11,620	812	--	--	--	--	
Beech	8,207	5,896	993	107	17	91,016	7,190	--	6	7	0	--	--	--	--	
White birch	6,585	7,494	1,316	1,461	238	59,357	4,689	--	--	4,893	342	--	--	--	--	
Yellow birch	4,070	9,175	1,545	1,063	173	28,294	2,235	--	--	1,672	117	--	--	--	--	
Other birch	4	25	4	--	--	--	--	--	--	--	--	--	--	--	--	
Black cherry	3,491	18,068	3,173	323	53	781	62	--	--	2,917	204	--	--	--	--	
Black walnut	792	4,211	709	328	53	--	--	0	--	418	29	--	--	--	--	
Cottonwood	365	1,798	316	--	--	47	4	--	22	338	24	--	--	--	--	
Elm	426	636	112	54	9	350	28	--	6	3,895	272	--	--	--	--	
Hickory	575	2,911	490	87	14	100	8	0	2	873	61	--	--	--	--	
Hard maple	59,887	152,616	24,754	12,143	1,977	379,274	29,963	--	51	44,951	3,142	--	--	--	--	
Soft maple	45,637	59,196	10,395	462	75	379,013	29,942	--	110	73,176	5,115	--	--	--	--	
Red oak group	20,805	74,969	13,157	4,125	671	28,554	2,256	4	135	65,531	4,581	--	--	--	--	0
White oak group	4,762	15,925	2,795	790	129	3,165	250	1	39	22,146	1,548	--	--	--	--	
Sycamore	138	108	19	11	2	--	--	--	0	1,667	117	--	--	--	--	
Yellow-poplar	253	1,323	232	79	13	--	--	--	7	2	0	--	--	--	--	
Other hardwoods	12,693	949	166	--	--	155,195	12,260	--	3	3,769	263	--	--	--	--	0
Hardwood total	240,591	444,142	75,648	30,669	4,993	1,754,333	138,592	6	465	298,793	20,886	--	--	--	--	1
State total	329,897	741,258	127,670	33,236	5,411	2,062,367	162,927	562	505	391,401	27,359	98,605	592	4,736	4,868	3

EASTERN UPPER PENINSULA

Species group	All products MCF[a]	Saw logs MBF[b]	Saw logs MCF[a]	Veneer logs MBF[b]	Veneer logs MCF[a]	Pulpwood Cords[c]	Pulpwood MCF[a]	Cabin logs MCF[a]	Excelsior/ shaving/ mulch MCF[2]	Industrial fuelwood Cords[c]	Industrial fuelwood MCF[a]	Poles Pieces	Poles MCF[a]	Posts M pieces[d]	Posts MCF[a]	Miscellaneous MCF[a]
Softwoods																
Northern white-cedar	3,045	2,832	533	--	--	602	48	199	--	--	--	--	--	2,203	2,265	--
Balsam fir	2,676	2,656	500	--	--	26,831	2,120	--	--	--	--	--	--	55	56	--
Hemlock	1,576	--	--	--	--	19,954	1,576	--	--	--	--	--	--	--	--	--
Jack pine	8,259	31,293	5,893	--	--	29,955	2,366	--	--	--	--	31,394	--	--	--	--
Red pine	5,110	21,637	3,628	40	7	15,923	1,258	29	--	--	--	--	188	--	--	--
White pine	631	1,767	296	103	17	3,862	305	13	--	--	--	--	--	--	--	--
Spruce	3,380	9,460	1,781	50	8	20,136	1,591	--	--	--	--	--	--	--	--	--
Tamarack	335	--	--	--	--	4,236	335	--	--	--	--	--	--	--	--	--
Softwood total	25,013	69,644	12,632	193	31	121,499	9,598	241	--	--	--	31,394	188	2,258	2,321	--
Hardwoods																
Ash	515	655	110	2	0	5,121	405	--	--	--	--	--	--	--	--	--
Aspen/balsam poplar	11,032	8,070	1,420	500	81	120,652	9,531	--	--	--	--	--	--	--	--	--
Basswood	798	1,514	266	30	5	6,679	528	--	--	--	--	--	--	--	--	--
Beech	3,709	2,860	482	--	--	40,855	3,228	--	--	--	--	--	--	--	--	--
White birch	2,349	3,438	604	434	71	21,195	1,674	--	--	--	--	--	--	--	--	--
Yellow birch	1,325	2,632	443	100	16	10,961	866	--	--	--	--	--	--	--	--	--
Black cherry	140	796	140	3	0	32	3	--	--	--	--	--	--	--	--	--
Elm	3	3	1	--	--	1	0	--	--	--	--	--	--	--	--	--
Hickory	0	--	--	--	--	--	--	--	--	--	--	--	--	--	--	--
Hard maple	14,552	26,129	4,238	1,907	310	126,627	10,004	--	--	--	--	--	--	--	--	--
Soft maple	11,337	11,750	2,063	38	6	117,307	9,267	--	--	--	--	--	--	--	--	--
Red oak group	644	1,902	334	101	16	3,719	294	--	--	--	--	--	--	--	--	--
White oak group	6	30	5	--	--	7	1	--	--	--	--	--	--	--	--	--
Other hardwoods	1,749	--	--	--	--	22,138	1,749	--	--	--	--	--	--	--	--	--
Hardwood total	48,161	59,780	10,105	3,115	507	475,294	37,548	--	--	--	--	--	--	--	--	--
Unit total	73,173	129,424	22,737	3,308	539	596,793	47,147	241	--	--	--	31,394	188	2,258	2,321	--

(Table 8 continued on next page)

39

(Table 8 continued)

WESTERN UPPER PENINSULA

Species group	All products MCF[a]	Saw logs MBF[b]	Saw logs MCF[a]	Veneer logs MBF[b]	Veneer logs MCF[a]	Pulpwood Cords[c]	Pulpwood MCF[a]	Cabin logs MCF[a]	Excelsior/shaving/mulch MCF[2]	Industrial fuelwood Cords[c]	Industrial fuelwood MCF[a]	Poles Pieces	Poles MCF[a]	Posts M pieces[d]	Posts MCF[a]	Miscellaneous MCF[a]
Softwoods																
Northern white-cedar	772	1,109	209	--	--	683	54	31	--	--	--	--	--	463	476	2
Balsam fir	2,979	3,877	730	--	--	28,111	2,221	--	--	--	--	--	--	28	28	--
Hemlock	2,799	221	37	--	--	34,959	2,762	--	--	--	--	--	--	--	--	--
Jack pine	4,920	16,986	3,198	--	--	21,794	1,722	--	--	--	--	--	--	--	--	--
Red pine	3,779	13,026	2,185	975	159	16,321	1,289	133	--	--	--	2,204	--	--	--	--
White pine	1,000	3,514	589	495	81	2,982	236	95	--	--	--	--	13	--	--	--
Spruce	4,169	10,886	2,050	833	136	25,088	1,982	2	--	--	--	--	--	--	--	--
Tamarack	602	--	--	--	--	7,624	602	--	--	--	--	--	--	--	--	--
Softwood total	21,021	49,619	8,998	2,303	375	137,562	10,867	261	--	--	--	2,204	13	491	505	2
Hardwoods																
Ash	1,210	1,749	294	36	6	11,518	910	--	--	--	--	--	--	--	--	--
Aspen/balsam poplar	13,038	6,365	1,119	8,633	1,405	133,079	10,513	--	--	--	--	--	--	--	--	--
Basswood	2,388	5,240	920	88	14	18,397	1,453	--	--	--	--	--	--	--	--	--
Beech	3,416	234	39	--	--	42,746	3,377	--	--	--	--	--	--	--	--	--
White birch	3,065	2,829	497	1,026	167	30,388	2,401	--	--	--	--	--	--	--	--	--
Yellow birch	2,563	6,281	1,058	927	151	17,144	1,354	--	--	--	--	--	--	--	--	--
River birch	4	25	4	--	--	--	--	--	--	--	--	--	--	--	--	--
Black cherry	197	1,096	193	26	4	--	--	--	--	--	--	--	--	--	--	--
Black walnut	2	--	--	14	2	--	--	--	--	--	--	--	--	--	--	--
Cottonwood	4	--	--	--	--	47	4	--	--	--	--	--	--	--	--	--
Elm	26	2	0	--	--	318	25	--	--	--	--	--	--	--	--	--
Hickory	13	28	5	--	--	99	8	--	--	--	--	--	--	--	--	--
Hard maple	22,387	44,240	7,176	4,462	726	183,352	14,485	--	--	--	--	--	--	--	--	--
Soft maple	14,888	12,939	2,272	396	65	158,876	12,551	--	--	--	--	--	--	--	--	--
Red oak group	1,921	4,880	856	2,420	394	8,491	671	--	--	--	--	--	--	--	--	--
White oak group	33	136	24	10	2	93	7	--	--	--	--	--	--	--	--	--
Other hardwoods	10,459	826	145	--	--	130,556	10,314	--	--	--	--	--	--	--	--	--
Hardwood total	75,613	86,869	14,603	18,038	2,937	735,104	58,073	--	--	--	--	--	--	--	--	--
Unit total	96,634	136,488	23,601	20,341	3,311	872,666	68,941	261	--	--	--	2,204	13	491	505	2

Species group	All products MCF[a]	Saw logs MBF[b]	Saw logs MCF[a]	Veneer logs MBF[b]	Veneer logs MCF[a]	Pulpwood Cords[c]	Pulpwood MCF[a]	Cabin logs MCF[a]	Excelsior/shaving/mulch MCF^2	Industrial fuelwood Cords[c]	Industrial fuelwood MCF[a]	Poles Pieces	Poles MCF[a]	Posts M pieces[d]	Posts MCF[a]	Miscellaneous MCF[a]
Softwoods																
Eastern redcedar	9	10	2	--	--	--	--	--	--	--	--	--	--	7	7	--
Northern white-cedar	855	2,264	426	--	--	2	0	--	--	--	--	--	--	417	429	--
Balsam fir	269	120	20	--	--	158	12	--	--	3,377	236	--	--	--	--	--
Hemlock	405	77	15	--	--	3,097	245	--	--	2,089	146	--	--	--	--	--
Jack pine	7,329	24,598	4,632	--	--	26,172	2,068	--	3	8,958	626	--	--	--	--	--
Red pine	29,572	135,407	22,708	--	--	12,768	1,009	34	21	55,021	3,846	58,546	351	1,560	1,604	--
White pine	1,588	3,862	648	71	12	689	54	--	11	12,311	861	--	--	3	3	--
Other pine	113	140	26	--	--	--	--	--	4	1,186	83	--	--	--	--	--
Spruce	513	199	37	--	--	3,876	306	--	--	2,428	170	--	--	--	--	--
Tamarack	69	--	--	--	--	17	1	--	--	968	68	--	--	--	--	--
Softwood total	40,723	166,677	28,514	71	12	46,778	3,695	34	40	86,336	6,035	58,546	351	1,987	2,042	--
Hardwoods																
Ash	3,400	9,786	1,648	159	26	7,392	584	--	10	16,196	1,132	--	--	--	--	--
Aspen/balsam poplar	32,451	36,056	6,342	5	1	298,982	23,620	--	27	35,212	2,461	--	--	--	--	--
Basswood	3,826	7,921	1,391	9	1	20,772	1,641	--	4	11,290	789	--	--	--	--	--
Beech	908	1,916	323	33	5	7,347	580	--	--	--	--	--	--	--	--	--
White birch	1,154	1,144	201	--	--	7,773	614	--	--	4,854	339	--	--	--	--	--
Yellow birch	166	234	39	31	5	190	15	--	--	1,518	106	--	--	--	--	--
Black cherry	867	4,470	785	132	21	769	61	--	--	--	--	--	--	--	--	--
Black walnut	5	31	5	--	--	--	--	--	--	--	--	--	--	--	--	--
Cottonwood	102	454	80	--	--	--	--	--	0	313	22	--	--	--	--	--
Elm	146	82	14	4	1	--	--	--	1	1,846	129	--	--	--	--	--
Hickory	34	130	22	3	1	--	--	--	--	165	12	--	--	--	--	--
Hard maple	20,325	71,049	11,524	2,101	342	68,797	5,435	--	10	43,112	3,014	--	--	--	--	--
Soft maple	15,081	20,687	3,633	372	61	101,448	8,014	--	26	48,745	3,407	--	--	--	--	--
Red oak group	12,970	46,389	8,141	54	9	16,344	1,291	--	28	49,345	3,449	--	--	--	--	--
White oak group	2,695	7,573	1,329	4	1	3,066	242	--	14	15,744	1,100	--	--	--	--	--
Yellow-poplar	2	7	1	--	--	--	--	--	--	--	--	--	--	--	--	--
Other hardwoods	196	3	1	--	--	2,465	195	--	--	13	--	--	--	--	--	--
Hardwood total	94,329	207,932	35,479	2,907	473	535,344	42,292	--	122	228,354	15,962	--	--	--	--	--
Unit total	135,051	374,609	63,993	2,978	485	582,121	45,988	34	162	314,689	21,997	58,546	351	1,987	2,042	--

(Table 8 continued on next page)

41

(Table 8 continued)

SOUTHERN LOWER PENINSULA

Species group	All products MCF[a]	Saw logs MBF[b]	Saw logs MCF[a]	Veneer logs MBF[b]	Veneer logs MCF[a]	Pulpwood Cords[c]	Pulpwood MCF[a]	Cabin logs MCF[a]	Excelsior/shaving/mulch MCF2	Industrial fuelwood Cords[c]	Industrial fuelwood MCF[a]	Poles Pieces	Poles MCF[a]	Posts M pieces[d]	Posts MCF[a]	Miscellaneous MCF[a]
Softwoods																
Eastern redcedar	1	--	--	--	--	--	--	1	--	--	--	--	--	--	--	--
Northern white-cedar	0	--	--	--	--	4	0	--	--	--	--	--	--	--	--	--
Balsam fir	9	--	--	--	--	115	9	--	--	--	--	--	--	--	--	--
Hemlock	10	--	--	--	--	126	10	--	--	--	--	--	--	--	--	--
Jack pine	164	154	29	--	--	1,539	122	--	--	189	13	--	--	--	--	--
Red pine	2,001	10,720	1,798	--	--	349	28	3	--	1,910	134	6,461	39	--	--	--
White pine	171	249	42	--	--	15	1	16	--	1,611	113	--	--	--	--	--
Other pine	189	52	10	--	--	--	--	--	0	2,562	179	--	--	--	--	--
Spruce	2	--	--	--	--	30	2	--	--	--	--	--	--	--	--	--
Tamarack	1	--	--	--	--	17	1	--	--	--	--	--	--	--	--	--
Softwood total	2,549	11,174	1,878	--	--	2,195	173	20	0	6,273	438	6,461	39	--	--	--
Hardwoods																
Ash	2,050	7,905	1,331	170	28	74	6	1	36	9,272	648	--	--	--	--	--
Aspen/balsam fir	849	1,840	324	--	--	6,442	509	--	--	238	17	--	--	--	--	--
Basswood	342	1,741	306	3	1	79	6	--	6	330	23	--	--	--	--	--
Beech	174	886	149	74	12	68	5	--	6	7	0	--	--	--	--	--
White birch	17	82	14	1	0	--	--	--	--	40	3	--	--	--	--	--
Yellow birch	16	28	5	6	1	--	--	--	--	154	11	--	--	--	--	--
Black cherry	2,287	11,705	2,055	163	26	12	1	--	--	2,917	204	--	--	--	--	--
Black walnut	784	4,180	704	314	51	--	--	0	--	418	29	--	--	--	--	--
Cottonwood	260	1,345	236	--	--	--	--	--	22	25	2	--	--	--	--	--
Elm	252	548	96	50	8	--	--	--	4	2,049	143	--	--	--	--	--
Hickory	529	2,753	464	84	14	--	--	0	2	707	49	--	--	--	--	--
Hard maple	2,623	11,199	1,816	3,673	598	498	39	--	41	1,839	129	--	--	--	--	--
Soft maple	4,332	13,820	2,427	27	4	1,382	109	--	83	24,431	1,708	--	--	--	--	--
Red oak group	5,269	21,798	3,826	1,232	201	--	--	4	107	16,187	1,131	--	--	--	--	0
White oak group	2,028	8,186	1,437	725	118	--	--	1	25	6,403	448	--	--	--	--	--
Sycamore	138	108	19	11	2	--	--	--	0	1,667	117	--	--	--	--	--
Yellow-poplar	251	1,316	231	75	12	--	--	--	7	2	0	--	--	--	--	--
Other hardwoods	288	119	7	--	--	35	3	--	3	3,755	262	--	--	--	--	0
Hardwood total	22,489	89,562	15,461	6,609	1,076	8,592	679	6	343	70,439	4,924	--	--	--	--	1
Unit total	25,038	100,736	17,339	6,609	1,076	10,787	852	26	343	76,712	5,362	6,461	39	--	--	1

[a] Thousand cubic feet.
[b] Thousand board feet, International 1/4-inch rule.
[c] Standard cords are 128 cubic feet consisting of 79 cubic feet of wood and 49 cubic feet of bark and air space.
[d] Thousand pieces.
All table cells without observations are indicated by --. Table value of 0 indicates the volume less than 1/2 unit of measure.
Columns and rows may not add to their totals due to rounding.

Table 9. -- Saw log receipts and production by Forest Inventory Unit and species group,
Michigan, 2004 and 2006

(In thousand board feet, International 1/4-inch rule)

ALL UNITS

Species group	Receipts			Production		
	2004	2006	Percent change	2004	2006	Percent change
Softwood						
Eastern redcedar	1	10	900%	--	10	--
Northern white-cedar	7,256	6,195	-15%	6,900	6,205	-10%
Balsam fir	11,457	7,965	-30%	8,971	6,610	-26%
Hemlock	1,684	1,504	-11%	402	342	-15%
Jack pine	105,088	88,904	-15%	71,171	73,030	3%
Red pine	161,083	198,157	23%	133,223	180,790	36%
White pine	13,443	9,377	-30%	12,173	9,391	-23%
Other pine	--	192	--	--	192	--
Spruce	24,946	25,999	4%	21,851	20,545	-6%
Tamarack	1,081	--	--	916	--	--
Total	326,039	338,302	4%	255,607	297,115	16%
Hardwood						
Ash	16,948	17,912	6%	18,755	20,094	7%
Aspen/balsam poplar	62,670	56,220	-10%	59,218	52,331	-12%
Basswood	16,932	13,495	-20%	18,768	16,417	-13%
Beech	11,531	6,401	-44%	8,922	5,896	-34%
White birch	6,995	7,009	0%	7,940	7,494	-6%
Yellow birch	6,842	7,767	14%	8,593	9,175	7%
Other birch	--	--	--	25	25	0%
Black cherry	17,134	15,866	-7%	19,153	18,068	-6%
Black walnut	2,115	3,424	62%	2,742	4,211	54%
Cottonwood	1,121	1,406	25%	1,569	1,798	15%
Elm	60	567	845%	314	636	103%
Hickory	2,565	2,278	-11%	4,223	2,911	-31%
Hard maple	113,757	150,013	32%	122,748	152,616	24%
Soft maple	50,613	58,088	15%	53,065	59,196	12%
Red oak group	87,857	73,373	-16%	89,634	74,969	-16%
White oak group	11,688	13,144	12%	14,522	15,925	10%

(Table 9 continued on next page)

(Table 9 continued)

Species	Receipts 2004	2006	Percent change	Production 2004	2006	Percent change
Sycamore	2	1	-50%	151	108	-28%
Yellow-poplar	400	363	-9%	1,243	1,323	6%
Other hardwoods	3	31	933%	996	949	-5%
Total	409,235	427,357	4%	432,581	444,142	3%
All species	735,274	765,659	4%	688,189	741,258	8%

EASTERN UPPER PENINSULA

Species group	Receipts 2004	2006	Percent change	Production 2004	2006	Percent change
Softwood						
Northern white-cedar	4,149	1,934	-53%	3,779	2,832	-25%
Balsam fir	--	3	--	2,301	2,656	15%
Hemlock	1,600	1,380	-14%	--	--	--
Jack pine	386	269	-30%	17,180	31,293	82%
Red pine	4,634	3,406	-26%	8,222	21,637	163%
White pine	7,096	4,244	-40%	4,169	1,767	-58%
Spruce	166	260	57%	3,578	9,460	164%
Tamarack	--	--	--	12	--	--
Total	18,030	11,496	-36%	39,240	69,644	77%
Hardwoods						
Ash	1,136	1,289	13%	660	655	-1%
Aspen/balsam poplar	9,000	8,312	-8%	7,351	8,070	10%
Basswood	3,636	1,525	-58%	2,098	1,514	-28%
Beech	7,180	3,708	-48%	3,682	2,860	-22%
White birch	2,159	1,829	-15%	3,793	3,438	-9%
Yellow birch	1,152	2,248	95%	2,127	2,632	24%
Black cherry	1,043	832	-20%	810	796	-2%
Elm	--	4	--	3	3	0%
Hard maple	12,545	33,060	164%	12,529	26,129	109%
Soft maple	7,167	13,355	86%	6,386	11,750	84%
Red oak group	4,476	2,371	-47%	1,634	1,902	16%
White oak group	432	--	--	462	30	-94%
Yellow-poplar	140	--	--	140	--	--
Total	50,064	68,533	37%	41,677	59,780	43%
All species	68,094	80,029	18%	80,917		-100%

WESTERN UPPER PENINSULA

Species group	Receipts			Production		
	2004	2006	Percent change	2004	2006	Percent change
Softwood						
Northern white-cedar	148	176	19%	1,866	1,109	-41%
Balsam fir	11,388	7,952	-30%	6,497	3,877	-40%
Hemlock	37	3	-92%	355	221	-38%
Jack pine	95,748	76,376	-20%	20,709	16,986	-18%
Red pine	47,424	48,245	2%	2,182	13,026	497%
White pine	3,311	1,022	-69%	4,275	3,514	-18%
Spruce	24,670	25,507	3%	17,883	10,886	-39%
Tamarack	1,081	0	-100%	294	--	--
Total	183,806	159,281	-13%	54,060	49,619	-8%
Hardwoods						
Ash	1,624	755	-54%	1,800	1,749	-3%
Aspen/balsam poplar	10,933	10,023	-8%	9,012	6,365	-29%
Basswood	2,782	2,685	-3%	5,366	5,240	-2%
Beech	24	--	--	369	234	-37%
White birch	3,618	4,120	14%	2,750	2,829	3%
Yellow birch	5,585	5,232	-6%	6,380	6,281	-2%
Other birch	--	--	--	25	25	0%
Black cherry	635	772	22%	846	1,096	30%
Elm	--	--	--	1	2	100%
Hickory	--	--	--	28	28	0%
Hard maple	34,513	33,315	-3%	41,809	44,240	6%
Soft maple	13,433	11,098	-17%	14,059	12,939	-8%
Red oak group	5,941	7,353	24%	5,694	4,880	-14%
White oak group	--	--	--	136	136	0%
Other hardwoods	--	--	--	826	826	0%
Total	79,088	75,352	-5%	89,099	86,869	-3%
All species	262,893	234,634	-11%	143,159	136,488	-5%

(Table 9 continued on next page)

45

(Table 9 continued)

NORTHERN LOWER PENINSULA

Species group	Receipts			Production		
	2004	2006	Percent change	2004	2006	Percent change
Softwood						
Eastern redcedar	1	10	900%	--	10	--
Northern white-cedar	2,959	4,070	38%	1,256	2,264	80%
Balsam fir	70	10	-86%	174	77	-56%
Hemlock	47	120	155%	37	120	224%
Jack pine	8,954	12,259	37%	33,281	24,598	-26%
Red pine	108,874	146,360	34%	119,660	135,407	13%
White pine	3,021	4,091	35%	3,592	3,862	8%
Other pine	--	192	--	--	140	--
Spruce	110	232	111%	391	199	-49%
Tamarack	--	--	--	610	--	--
Total	124,036	167,345	35%	159,000	166,677	5%
Hardwoods						
Ash	7,882	9,637	22%	8,033	9,786	22%
Aspen/balsam poplar	37,825	33,674	-11%	40,522	36,056	-11%
Beech	3,631	1,803	-50%	3,563	1,916	-46%
Basswood	8,632	7,706	-11%	8,570	7,921	-8%
White birch	1,082	847	-22%	1,339	1,144	-15%
Yellow birch	96	264	175%	82	234	185%
Black cherry	3,853	4,646	21%	3,088	4,470	45%
Black walnut	174	247	42%	49	31	-37%
Cottonwood	255	206	-19%	521	454	-13%
Elm	30	37	23%	34	82	141%
Hickory	809	655	-19%	411	130	-68%
Hard maple	46,242	58,359	26%	51,788	71,049	37%
Soft maple	18,346	20,276	11%	19,476	20,687	6%
Red oak group	47,015	43,616	-7%	48,286	46,389	-4%
White oak group	5,179	7,378	42%	5,293	7,573	43%
Other hardwoods	--	--	--	3	3	0%
Yellow-poplar	123	1	-99%	53	7	-87%
Total	181,173	189,351	5%	191,110	207,932	9%
All species	305,209	356,696	17%	350,110	374,609	7%

SOUTHERN LOWER PENINSULA

Species group	Receipts			Production		
	2004	2006	Percent change	2004	2006	Percent change
Softwood						
Hemlock	--	--	--	10	--	--
Jack pine	--	--	--	2	154	7600%
Red pine	152	146	-4%	3,159	10,720	239%
White pine	16	19	19%	137	249	82%
Other pine	--	15	--	--	--	--
Total	168	180	7%	3,308	11,174	238%
Hardwoods						
Ash	6,307	6,232	-1%	8,261	7,905	-4%
Aspen/balsam poplar	4,912	4,211	-14%	2,332	1,840	-21%
Basswood	1,883	1,580	-16%	2,733	1,741	-36%
Beech	696	890	28%	1,309	886	-32%
White birch	136	213	57%	58	82	41%
Yellow birch	10	24	140%	4	28	600%
Black cherry	11,603	9,616	-17%	14,410	11,705	-19%
Black walnut	1,941	3,177	64%	2,694	4,180	55%
Cottonwood	867	1,200	38%	1,048	1,345	28%
Elm	30	526	1653%	276	548	99%
Hickory	1,756	1,623	-8%	3,784	2,753	-27%
Hard maple	20,456	25,279	24%	16,622	11,199	-33%
Soft maple	11,668	13,359	14%	13,143	13,820	5%
Red oak group	30,426	20,033	-34%	34,021	21,798	-36%
White oak group	6,077	5,765	-5%	8,631	8,186	-5%
Other hardwoods	2	31	1450%	167	119	-29%
Sycamore	2	1	-50%	151	108	-28%
Yellow-poplar	137	362	164%	1,050	1,316	25%
Total	98,910	94,120	-5%	110,695	89,562	-19%
All species	99,078	94,300	-5%	114,003	100,736	-12%

All table cells without observations are indicated by --. Table value of 0 indicates the volume rounds to less than 1 thousand board feet. Columns and rows may not add to their totals due to rounding.

47

Table 10.-- Wood material harvested for industrial roundwood by Forest Inventory Unit, source of material, and species group, Michigan, 2006[a]

(In thousand cubic feet)

ALL UNITS

	Source of material												
	Growing stock				Non-growing stock								
	Used for products		Logging residue (not used)	Total growing stock	Used for products				Logging slash (not used)	Total non growing stock	Total used	Total not used	Total harvested
Species group	Sawtimber	Pole-timber			Limbwood	Saplings	Cull trees	Dead trees					
Softwoods													
Eastern redcedar	4.2	4.7	1.2	10.0	0.3	0.4	0.1	0.1	1.4	2.2	9.7	2.5	12.2
Northern white-cedar	2,144.7	2,161.3	547.1	4,853.0	131.3	162.5	42.3	30.9	728.1	1,095.1	4,672.9	1,275.2	5,948.1
Balsam fir	4,421.1	1,306.2	338.5	6,065.8	216.1	57.1	24.5	44.5	1,912.0	2,254.3	6,069.5	2,250.5	8,320.0
Hemlock	2,359.8	1,490.0	140.3	3,990.2	337.4	105.5	239.1	121.9	1,375.4	2,179.3	4,653.8	1,515.7	6,169.6
Jack pine	16,218.8	2,739.9	1,671.8	20,630.5	911.9	113.1	134.2	553.7	6,979.9	8,692.8	20,671.6	8,651.7	29,323.3
Red pine	33,166.8	3,964.0	1,676.0	38,806.8	2,332.3	179.2	447.4	372.8	10,404.9	13,736.5	40,462.4	12,080.9	52,543.2
White pine	2,280.9	519.0	109.2	2,909.0	447.5	17.3	94.5	31.8	744.5	1,335.5	3,390.9	853.7	4,244.5
Other pine	101.0	80.8	4.6	186.4	104.8	0.7	14.4	0.8	20.8	141.5	302.4	25.4	327.9
Spruce	6,485.7	1,114.7	609.7	8,210.1	275.5	44.7	45.4	99.0	2,738.6	3,203.2	8,065.0	3,348.3	11,413.3
Tamarack	672.1	262.9	39.3	974.2	51.8	10.9	6.1	3.6	293.1	365.4	1,007.3	332.4	1,339.7
Softwood total	67,855.1	13,643.3	5,137.6	86,636.1	4,808.7	691.3	1,048.0	1,259.0	25,198.7	33,005.8	89,305.5	30,336.3	119,641.8
Hardwoods													
Ash	4,497.4	1,019.0	521.4	6,037.8	969.6	11.0	676.1	1.9	1,377.8	3,036.3	7,174.9	1,899.2	9,074.1
Aspen/balsam poplar	27,065.7	25,996.4	2,682.4	55,744.4	2,119.2	26.8	1,811.9	351.3	10,179.6	14,488.8	57,371.3	12,861.9	70,233.2
Basswood	4,177.1	2,146.3	665.1	6,988.6	635.8	13.4	326.5	55.1	1,295.9	2,326.7	7,354.2	1,961.1	9,315.3
Beech	3,949.3	1,430.5	523.9	5,903.7	742.9	5.4	2,077.7	1.7	2,796.4	5,624.1	8,207.5	3,320.3	11,527.8
White birch	3,142.3	2,456.4	530.2	6,128.9	508.7	12.9	393.5	71.2	1,253.2	2,239.5	6,585.0	1,783.4	8,368.4
Yellow birch	2,587.4	480.7	338.1	3,406.1	302.3	0.4	699.5	0.0	1,173.8	2,176.0	4,070.3	1,511.8	5,582.1
Other birch	4.1	0.2	0.7	4.9	0.1	—	0.0	—	0.9	0.9	4.4	1.5	5.9
Black cherry	3,107.0	217.4	492.0	3,816.4	126.3	1.6	37.7	0.9	650.1	816.6	3,490.9	1,142.1	4,633.0
Black walnut	727.0	19.7	92.4	839.1	26.4	0.1	18.6	—	154.3	199.4	791.8	246.7	1,038.5
Cottonwood	321.2	27.2	54.2	402.6	13.6	0.1	3.4	0.1	63.7	80.8	365.5	118.0	483.4
Elm	194.1	100.9	21.7	316.7	111.4	0.9	18.3	0.4	36.8	167.9	426.0	58.5	484.5
Hickory	496.9	27.8	61.0	585.7	35.2	0.2	15.1	0.0	104.3	154.8	575.2	165.3	740.5
Hard maple	38,430.1	7,451.2	5,389.5	51,270.8	4,892.8	48.4	9,051.8	12.7	16,607.3	30,613.0	59,887.0	21,996.8	81,883.8
Soft maple	21,366.1	16,736.6	3,447.4	41,550.0	4,452.7	108.4	2,518.7	454.3	7,992.4	15,526.5	45,636.8	11,439.7	57,076.6
Red oak group	14,025.6	3,355.3	1,445.4	18,826.3	2,428.3	56.6	664.3	274.7	2,270.2	5,694.0	20,804.8	3,715.6	24,520.4
White oak group	3,079.1	743.4	300.4	4,122.8	717.1	11.6	160.2	50.3	459.8	1,399.0	4,761.7	760.2	5,521.9
Sycamore	48.8	35.7	3.3	87.7	46.4	0.3	6.6	—	7.3	60.6	137.8	10.6	148.4
Yellow-poplar	236.0	11.0	39.4	286.3	3.0	0.0	2.6	—	49.3	54.9	252.6	88.7	341.2
Other hardwoods	4,402.9	6,117.6	782.5	11,302.9	1,040.8	34.4	911.8	186.2	2,434.5	4,607.5	12,693.8	3,216.8	15,910.5
Hardwood total	131,857.9	68,373.2	17,390.9	217,622.0	19,172.6	332.2	19,394.5	1,460.8	48,907.4	89,267.5	240,591.3	66,298.2	306,889.5
State total	199,713.1	82,016.5	22,528.5	304,258.1	23,981.4	1,023.5	20,442.5	2,719.8	74,106.1	122,273.3	329,896.8	96,634.6	426,531.4

EASTERN UPPER PENINSULA

Source of material

	Growing stock				Non-growing stock								
	Used for products		Logging residue (not used)	Total growing stock	Used for products			Dead trees	Logging slash (not used)	Total non growing stock	Total used	Total not used	Total harvested
Species group	Sawtimber	Pole-timber			Limbwood	Saplings	Cull trees						
Softwoods													
Northern white-cedar	1,265.1	1,532.9	360.4	3,158.3	85.9	115.8	29.3	16.1	409.5	656.6	3,045.1	769.9	3,815.0
Balsam fir	1,958.1	592.7	150.1	2,700.9	71.5	27.0	7.6	18.9	852.7	977.8	2,675.9	1,002.8	3,678.7
Hemlock	812.1	512.8	49.9	1,374.8	87.8	37.9	81.8	43.9	488.9	740.3	1,576.3	538.7	2,115.1
Jack pine	6,714.2	971.6	707.6	8,393.3	267.4	41.9	39.7	224.2	2,897.8	3,471.1	8,259.0	3,605.4	11,864.4
Red pine	4,331.2	480.7	216.5	5,028.4	131.1	30.3	69.1	67.7	1,482.1	1,780.3	5,110.1	1,698.6	6,808.7
White pine	468.9	104.2	25.2	598.4	22.2	7.3	17.5	11.3	191.1	249.3	631.4	216.3	847.7
Spruce	2,777.1	439.2	262.7	3,478.9	90.5	18.1	10.5	44.8	1,181.5	1,345.5	3,380.2	1,444.2	4,824.4
Tamarack	233.4	86.4	14.0	333.8	8.9	3.8	0.8	1.3	103.8	118.6	334.7	117.8	452.5
Softwood total	18,560.1	4,720.4	1,786.4	25,066.9	765.4	282.2	256.4	428.2	7,607.4	9,339.5	25,012.7	9,393.7	34,406.5
Hardwoods													
Ash	274.8	78.0	36.1	388.9	42.8	--	119.7	--	170.2	332.6	515.3	206.2	721.5
Aspen/balsam poplar	5,032.0	5,385.8	499.1	10,916.9	200.5	--	340.2	74.0	2,058.7	2,673.4	11,032.4	2,557.9	13,590.3
Basswood	435.5	269.4	73.8	778.8	43.4	1.3	40.7	8.0	157.0	250.5	798.4	230.8	1,029.3
Beech	1,812.5	616.2	240.5	2,669.2	332.8	--	947.7	--	1,278.9	2,559.3	3,709.1	1,519.4	5,228.5
White birch	1,205.3	845.8	207.2	2,258.2	134.9	4.2	133.3	25.4	466.6	764.5	2,348.8	673.8	3,022.7
Yellow birch	798.3	170.2	104.2	1,072.6	95.8	--	261.1	--	409.0	765.9	1,325.4	513.2	1,838.5
Black cherry	132.3	5.4	21.3	158.9	1.8	--	0.8	--	27.5	30.1	140.3	48.8	189.0
Elm	1.4	1.3	0.2	2.9	0.2	0.0	0.2	0.0	0.6	1.0	3.1	0.8	3.9
Hickory	0.0	0.0	0.0	0.1	0.0	--	0.0	--	0.0	0.1	0.1	0.0	0.1
Hard maple	8,504.8	1,959.9	1,202.1	11,666.8	1,108.1	--	2,979.3	--	4,663.4	8,750.8	14,552.1	5,865.5	20,417.6
Soft maple	5,118.8	4,631.4	888.4	10,638.6	729.7	23.5	692.7	140.8	2,224.2	3,810.9	11,336.8	3,112.6	14,449.5
Red oak group	363.1	197.6	44.4	605.1	42.6	1.9	22.8	16.1	93.7	177.1	644.0	138.1	782.1
White oak group	4.8	0.6	0.5	5.9	0.2	0.0	0.1	0.1	0.8	1.2	5.8	1.3	7.1
Other hardwoods	597.7	858.9	108.5	1,565.1	132.8	4.4	128.4	26.6	343.1	635.4	1,748.9	451.6	2,200.5
Hardwood total	24,281.3	15,020.4	3,426.3	42,728.0	2,865.5	35.3	5,667.0	291.0	11,893.8	20,752.7	48,160.5	15,320.1	63,480.6
Unit total	42,841.4	19,740.9	5,212.7	67,794.9	3,630.9	317.5	5,923.4	719.3	19,501.2	30,092.2	73,173.2	24,713.9	97,887.1

(Table 10 continued on next page)

49

(Table 10 continued)

WESTERN UPPER PENINSULA

Species group	Source of material										Total used	Total not used	Total harvested
	Growing stock				Non-growing stock								
	Used for products		Logging residue (not used)	Total growing stock	Used for products				Logging slash (not used)	Total non growing stock			
	Sawtimber	Pole-timber			Limbwood	Saplings	Cull trees	Dead trees					
Softwoods													
Northern white-cedar	378.0	335.8	87.3	801.1	21.6	24.9	6.6	5.4	133.0	191.4	772.2	220.3	992.5
Balsam fir	1,458.4	899.0	88.9	2,446.4	154.4	66.4	143.3	77.2	867.5	1,308.9	2,798.9	956.4	3,755.3
Hemlock	2,236.3	604.1	176.1	3,016.5	79.6	26.7	8.3	24.3	971.2	1,110.2	2,979.4	1,147.4	4,126.7
Jack pine	3,870.1	689.5	395.7	4,955.3	165.1	30.5	25.4	139.4	1,689.1	2,049.5	4,920.1	2,084.8	7,004.9
Red pine	3,040.5	457.7	164.7	3,662.8	110.8	31.0	82.6	56.6	1,131.8	1,412.9	3,779.2	1,296.5	5,075.7
White pine	849.4	87.7	49.2	986.2	24.7	5.7	20.1	12.7	298.4	361.6	1,000.2	347.6	1,347.8
Spruce	3,416.5	544.5	330.0	4,291.0	108.5	22.6	24.8	52.2	1,442.6	1,650.7	4,169.0	1,772.6	5,941.7
Tamarack	420.1	155.5	25.2	600.8	16.0	6.9	1.5	2.3	186.8	213.5	602.3	211.9	814.2
Softwood total	15,669.2	3,773.8	1,317.1	20,760.1	680.7	214.6	312.7	370.2	6,720.5	8,298.7	21,021.2	8,037.6	29,058.8
Hardwoods													
Ash	666.4	176.4	87.4	930.2	97.1	0.0	270.2	0.0	393.0	760.4	1,210.2	480.4	1,690.7
Aspen/balsam poplar	6,356.0	5,870.0	730.7	12,960.8	225.2	0.9	500.8	81.4	2,542.8	3,351.0	13,038.3	3,273.5	16,311.8
Basswood	1,377.4	749.4	231.9	2,358.7	121.9	3.7	113.3	22.1	469.4	730.5	2,387.8	701.4	3,089.2
Beech	1,456.4	637.5	197.0	2,290.9	338.5	--	983.8	--	1,247.3	2,569.7	3,416.3	1,444.3	4,860.6
White birch	1,439.2	1,198.5	252.2	2,889.9	188.9	6.1	195.3	36.5	615.1	1,041.9	3,064.5	867.3	3,931.8
Yellow birch	4.1	0.2	0.7	4.9	0.1	--	0.0	--	0.9	0.9	4.4	1.5	5.9
River birch	1,706.6	272.1	226.9	2,205.6	157.7	0.0	426.5	0.0	745.9	1,330.1	2,562.9	972.8	3,535.7
Black cherry	185.4	7.5	29.9	222.7	2.4	--	1.5	--	38.9	42.8	196.8	68.8	265.5
Black walnut	2.0	--	0.4	2.4	0.0	--	0.2	--	0.6	0.8	2.2	1.0	3.2
Cottonwood	1.3	1.8	0.2	3.3	0.3	0.0	0.3	0.1	0.7	1.3	3.7	1.0	4.7
Elm	8.9	12.4	1.6	22.9	1.9	0.1	1.8	0.4	5.0	9.2	25.5	6.6	32.1
Hickory	7.7	1.6	1.0	10.3	0.9	0.0	2.3	0.0	3.8	7.0	12.5	4.8	17.3
Hard maple	13,549.0	2,857.4	1,929.3	18,335.6	1,631.3	0.1	4,349.0	0.0	7,050.6	13,031.2	22,386.9	8,979.9	31,366.8
Soft maple	6,489.9	6,252.8	1,133.4	13,876.0	982.0	31.9	940.6	190.6	2,925.4	5,070.4	14,887.7	4,058.7	18,946.5
Red oak group	1,234.5	455.3	169.4	1,859.2	100.7	5.1	87.9	37.7	323.3	554.7	1,921.2	492.7	2,413.9
White oak group	24.1	5.6	2.6	32.4	1.5	0.2	0.9	0.5	4.1	7.3	32.9	6.8	39.7
Other hardwoods	3,661.8	5,071.2	661.7	9,394.7	785.1	26.1	758.0	156.7	2,052.1	3,778.0	10,459.0	2,713.7	13,172.7
Hardwood total	38,174.8	23,569.6	5,656.3	67,400.7	4,635.5	74.3	8,632.7	526.0	18,418.9	32,287.4	75,612.9	24,075.2	99,688.1
Unit total	53,844.1	27,343.3	6,973.4	88,160.7	5,316.2	288.9	8,945.3	896.2	25,139.4	40,586.1	96,634.1	32,112.8	128,746.8

50

NORTHERN LOWER PENINSULA

	Source of material												
	Growing stock				Non-growing stock								
	Used for products		Logging residue (not used)	Total growing stock	Used for products				Logging slash (not used)	Total non growing stock	Total used	Total not used	Total harvested
Species group	Sawtimber	Pole-timber			Limbwood	Saplings	Cull trees	Dead trees					
Softwoods													
Eastern redcedar	3.5	4.7	1.1	9.2	0.3	0.4	0.1	0.0	1.1	1.8	8.9	2.1	11.0
Northern white-cedar	501.5	292.5	99.3	893.3	23.8	21.8	6.4	9.3	185.6	246.9	855.3	284.9	1,140.2
Balsam fir	220.3	107.1	11.8	339.2	64.8	3.2	8.6	1.2	85.2	163.1	405.2	97.1	502.3
Hemlock	84.2	74.9	1.2	160.3	94.6	1.0	13.5	0.5	15.9	125.5	268.7	17.1	285.8
Jack pine	5,541.5	1,029.3	562.2	7,133.0	467.8	38.4	67.1	184.6	2,349.2	3,107.1	7,328.8	2,911.3	10,240.1
Red pine	23,986.3	2,945.2	1,214.7	28,146.2	2,005.8	116.9	286.3	231.5	7,243.8	9,884.3	29,572.0	8,458.5	38,030.6
White pine	878.9	292.1	32.4	1,203.3	354.9	3.9	50.8	7.3	234.7	651.6	1,587.9	267.0	1,854.9
Other pine	47.5	27.1	3.5	78.1	33.6	0.2	4.6	0.6	12.4	51.4	113.5	16.0	129.5
Spruce	290.5	130.4	16.9	437.8	76.4	4.0	10.1	2.0	113.8	206.2	513.4	130.6	644.0
Tamarack	17.7	20.6	0.1	38.3	26.8	0.2	3.7	0.0	2.2	32.9	69.0	2.2	71.2
Softwood total	31,571.8	4,923.8	1,943.2	38,438.8	3,148.7	190.0	451.2	437.1	10,243.8	14,470.8	40,722.6	12,187.0	52,909.6
Hardwoods													
Ash	2,080.4	539.3	226.3	2,846.0	544.6	9.1	224.4	1.9	526.8	1,306.8	3,399.6	753.2	4,152.8
Aspen/balsam poplar	15,198.3	14,411.4	1,405.0	31,014.8	1,672.9	25.9	951.2	191.7	5,421.0	8,262.6	32,451.3	6,826.0	39,277.3
Basswood	2,063.3	1,104.0	310.9	3,478.2	457.0	8.3	168.9	24.9	607.5	1,266.6	3,826.4	918.4	4,744.9
Beech	521.1	171.6	64.8	757.5	67.8	5.4	140.9	1.7	235.5	451.3	908.5	300.3	1,208.8
White birch	483.3	410.8	68.5	962.7	183.6	2.5	64.7	9.3	168.6	428.7	1,154.3	237.1	1,391.4
Yellow birch	74.4	35.2	6.3	115.9	44.4	0.3	11.3	--	17.3	73.3	165.5	23.7	189.2
Black cherry	776.4	63.5	125.0	964.9	15.5	1.0	9.9	0.9	168.2	195.5	867.2	293.2	1,160.4
Black walnut	5.0	0.1	0.6	5.7	0.1	--	0.1	--	1.0	1.2	5.3	1.6	6.9
Cottonwood	80.9	9.7	12.2	102.8	9.7	0.1	1.6	--	16.2	27.6	102.0	28.4	130.4
Elm	47.2	39.6	2.7	89.5	51.3	0.4	7.2	--	6.4	65.2	145.6	9.1	154.7
Hickory	24.1	3.8	2.7	30.5	5.0	0.0	1.0	--	4.7	10.8	34.0	7.4	41.4
Hard maple	14,036.1	2,545.5	1,895.3	18,476.9	2,051.6	47.9	1,630.9	12.7	4,319.2	8,062.2	20,324.7	6,214.5	26,539.1
Soft maple	6,944.2	5,171.5	1,027.3	13,143.1	2,025.7	47.9	770.3	121.2	2,298.8	5,263.8	15,080.8	3,326.1	18,406.9
Red oak group	8,447.9	2,184.4	805.9	11,438.2	1,735.9	46.3	396.1	159.7	1,267.6	3,605.7	12,970.4	2,073.4	15,043.8
White oak group	1,523.2	540.1	134.5	2,197.8	500.2	10.1	94.7	26.7	222.9	854.6	2,695.0	357.4	3,052.3
Yellow-poplar	1.8	0.0	0.3	2.1	0.0	--	0.1	--	0.4	0.5	1.9	0.7	2.6
Other hardwoods	55.2	106.0	8.2	169.4	18.3	3.1	10.8	2.9	27.6	62.7	196.3	35.8	232.1
Hardwood total	52,362.9	27,336.5	6,096.5	85,795.9	9,383.4	208.2	4,484.1	553.7	15,309.6	29,939.1	94,328.8	21,406.2	115,734.9
Unit total	83,934.7	32,260.3	8,039.7	124,234.6	12,532.2	398.2	4,935.3	990.7	25,553.5	44,409.9	135,051.3	33,593.1	168,644.5

(Table 10 continued on next page)

(Table 10 continued)

SOUTHERN LOWER PENINSULA

	Source of material												
	Growing stock				Non-growing stock								
	Used for products		Logging residue (not used)	Total growing stock	Used for products				Logging slash (not used)	Total non growing stock	Total used	Total not used	Total harvested
Species group	Sawtimber	Pole-timber			Limbwood	Saplings	Cull trees	Dead trees					
Softwoods													
Eastern redcedar	0.7	0.0	0.1	0.8	0.0	--	0.0	0.0	0.3	0.3	0.8	0.4	1.2
Northern white-cedar	0.2	0.1	0.0	0.3	0.0	0.0	0.0	0.0	0.1	0.1	0.3	0.1	0.4
Balsam fir	6.4	2.4	0.4	9.1	0.2	0.1	0.0	0.0	2.8	3.2	9.1	3.2	12.3
Hemlock	5.1	3.2	0.3	8.7	0.6	0.2	0.5	0.3	3.1	4.7	10.0	3.4	13.4
Jack pine	93.0	49.5	6.4	148.9	11.6	2.2	1.9	5.6	43.8	65.0	163.7	50.2	213.9
Red pine	1,808.8	80.5	80.2	1,969.4	84.5	1.0	9.3	16.9	547.1	658.9	2,001.1	627.2	2,628.3
White pine	83.6	35.0	2.4	121.0	45.7	0.4	6.2	0.5	20.3	73.1	171.4	22.7	194.1
Other pine	53.5	53.7	1.1	108.3	71.2	0.5	9.8	0.2	8.4	90.1	188.9	9.5	198.4
Spruce	1.7	0.6	0.1	2.4	0.1	0.0	0.0	0.0	0.7	0.8	2.4	0.8	3.2
Tamarack	0.9	0.3	0.1	1.3	0.0	0.0	0.0	0.0	0.4	0.5	1.3	0.5	1.8
Softwood total	2,054.0	225.3	91.0	2,370.3	213.9	4.5	27.7	23.5	627.1	896.7	2,549.0	718.1	3,267.0
Hardwoods													
Ash	1,475.7	225.3	171.6	1,872.7	285.1	1.9	61.8	--	287.7	636.5	2,049.8	459.3	2,509.2
Aspen/balsam poplar	475.3	329.2	47.5	852.0	20.7	0.0	19.8	4.2	157.0	201.8	849.2	204.5	1,053.8
Basswood	301.0	23.4	48.4	372.9	13.4	0.1	3.5	0.1	62.0	79.1	341.5	110.4	452.0
Beech	159.3	5.2	21.7	186.1	3.8	0.0	5.2	--	34.7	43.8	173.5	56.3	229.9
White birch	14.4	1.4	2.2	18.0	1.3	0.0	0.2	--	2.9	4.5	17.4	5.2	22.5
Yellow birch	8.0	3.3	0.7	12.0	4.4	0.0	0.8	--	1.5	6.6	16.5	2.2	18.7
Black cherry	2,013.0	141.0	315.9	2,469.8	106.7	0.6	25.4	0.0	415.5	548.2	2,286.7	731.4	3,018.1
Black walnut	720.1	19.6	91.4	831.1	26.3	0.1	18.3	--	152.7	197.3	784.4	244.0	1,028.4
Cottonwood	239.0	15.6	41.8	296.5	3.7	0.0	1.4	--	46.8	51.9	259.7	88.6	348.4
Elm	136.6	47.7	17.1	201.4	58.0	0.4	9.1	--	24.9	92.4	251.8	42.0	293.8
Hickory	465.1	22.4	57.3	544.8	29.3	0.1	11.7	--	95.8	136.9	528.6	153.1	681.7
Hard maple	2,340.2	88.4	362.9	2,791.4	101.9	0.4	92.5	--	574.1	768.9	2,623.3	936.9	3,560.3
Soft maple	2,813.2	680.9	398.2	3,892.4	715.4	5.2	115.1	1.7	544.0	1,381.4	4,331.5	942.3	5,273.8
Red oak group	3,980.1	518.0	425.7	4,923.9	549.1	3.2	157.5	61.1	585.6	1,356.6	5,269.1	1,011.4	6,280.5
White oak group	1,526.9	197.1	162.7	1,886.8	215.2	1.3	64.5	22.9	232.0	536.0	2,028.0	394.7	2,422.8
Sycamore	48.8	35.7	3.3	87.7	46.4	0.3	6.6	--	7.3	60.6	137.8	10.6	148.4
Yellow-poplar	234.2	11.0	39.1	284.2	3.0	0.0	2.5	--	48.9	54.4	250.7	87.9	338.6
Other hardwoods	88.2	81.4	4.2	173.7	104.5	0.8	14.5	0.0	11.7	131.5	289.6	15.6	305.3
Hardwood total	17,039.0	2,446.8	2,211.8	21,697.5	2,288.2	14.4	610.7	90.1	3,285.0	6,288.4	22,489.2	5,496.7	27,985.9
Unit total	19,093.0	2,672.1	2,302.7	24,067.8	2,502.1	18.9	638.5	113.6	3,912.0	7,185.1	25,038.1	6,214.8	31,252.9

[a] Based on factors obtained from regional utilization studies.

All table cells without observations are indicated by -- . Table value of 0.0 indicates the volume rounds to less than 0.1 thousand cubic feet. Columns and rows may not add to their totals due to rounding.

Table 11.-- Growing-stock removals from timberland for industrial roundwood by Forest Inventory Unit, county, and species group, Michigan, 2006

(In thousand cubic feet)

Forest inventory Unit and county	All species	Softwoods											Hardwoods			
		Eastern red-cedar	Northern white-cedar	Balsam fir	Hemlock	Jack pine	Red pine	White pine	Other pine	Spruce	Tama-rack	Total softwoods	Ash	Aspen/balsam poplar	Bass-wood	Beech
Eastern Upper Peninsula																
Alger	11,527	--	69	315	292	490	1,033	266	--	311	41	2,817	64	3,283	79	499
Chippewa	8,758	--	174	393	163	2,656	750	50	--	873	11	5,070	39	851	30	201
Delta	10,963	--	845	453	223	993	867	74	--	415	59	3,929	80	1,403	148	433
Luce	10,890	--	156	387	194	2,013	447	57	--	705	36	3,995	61	1,146	61	607
Mackinac	7,383	--	156	277	52	441	850	47	--	455	18	2,297	42	1,709	94	227
Menominee	9,898	--	1,602	617	351	254	292	67	--	419	138	3,739	51	1,358	272	325
Schoolcraft	8,376	--	157	258	100	1,545	791	38	--	300	31	3,220	52	1,166	96	377
Total	67,795	--	3,158	2,701	1,375	8,393	5,028	598	--	3,479	334	25,067	389	10,917	779	2,669
Western Upper Peninsula																
Baraga	11,463	--	46	307	432	457	295	46	--	370	41	1,994	106	1,818	261	518
Dickinson	8,945	--	189	440	92	329	333	102	--	615	120	2,221	59	1,400	443	190
Gogebic	8,508	--	28	140	108	16	400	51	--	336	15	1,094	200	982	242	92
Houghton	10,109	--	66	174	295	686	499	10	--	268	27	2,025	126	1,398	297	164
Iron	12,644	--	69	697	183	503	696	88	--	1,104	166	3,505	108	1,573	420	159
Keweenaw	4,438	--	35	86	52	18	38	5	--	118	8	360	81	219	110	121
Marquette	22,868	--	194	956	961	2,800	1,064	617	--	1,108	193	7,895	88	3,543	264	895
Ontonagon	9,186	--	174	216	324	146	337	67	--	372	30	1,667	162	2,028	321	152
Total	88,161	--	801	3,017	2,446	4,955	3,663	986	--	4,291	601	20,760	930	12,961	2,359	2,291
Northern Lower Peninsula																
Alcona	5,478	--	79	4	2	177	697	35	0	12	1	1,006	209	2,569	56	14
Alpena	3,622	7	240	32	18	59	413	36	1	52	3	860	149	1,554	72	13
Antrim	4,301	--	8	0	--	32	439	1	2	0	--	482	175	601	500	54
Arenac	950	0	2	0	1	107	38	16	--	0	--	166	52	292	10	5
Bay	275	--	--	--	1	2	--	1	--	--	--	4	17	102	15	--
Benzie	3,207	--	--	--	7	50	584	7	--	0	--	648	85	386	79	32
Charlevoix	2,587	--	41	5	4	1	301	21	--	5	4	382	110	470	321	38
Cheboygan	5,112	--	65	45	4	351	953	61	0	66	6	1,552	90	1,787	235	29
Clare	5,396	--	12	1	3	263	871	11	--	0	1	1,163	69	2,479	22	25
Crawford	5,904	--	8	1	2	1,163	1,642	33	1	8	1	2,860	13	1,317	67	10
Emmet	3,161	--	19	6	2	31	285	17	5	7	3	374	190	623	245	19
Gladwin	2,811	--	2	0	0	72	331	13	--	0	0	418	59	1,301	29	15
Grand Traverse	3,935	--	15	1	5	83	1,495	73	4	2	4	1,681	72	289	89	16
Iosco	4,379	1	23	8	4	591	2,087	50	--	6	2	2,774	51	610	17	6
Isabella	1,768	--	--	--	1	8	113	3	4	--	1	129	93	732	50	4
Kalkaska	6,740	--	12	5	6	392	2,497	61	6	2	1	2,980	79	923	273	44
Lake	4,778	--	12	--	5	566	1,549	67	1	2	1	2,203	36	533	35	27
Leelanau	1,890	--	--	1	16	16	160	26	0	0	2	222	119	100	68	26
Manistee	6,205	--	--	0	7	151	1,690	62	1	--	0	1,911	138	987	73	88
Mason	3,217	--	3	0	9	108	904	26	2	0	--	1,053	39	672	19	24
Mecosta	2,664	--	--	0	16	21	377	103	18	5	0	541	70	997	23	21
Midland	1,241	--	--	--	--	5	12	53	0	--	--	71	97	392	23	2
Missaukee	4,014	--	14	3	6	164	1,063	22	2	4	3	1,281	71	1,254	132	11
Montmorency	4,601	--	19	77	2	331	580	94	1	79	1	1,183	50	1,718	217	20
Newaygo	3,945	--	--	--	7	237	653	59	10	--	--	965	96	366	40	18
Oceana	2,238	--	--	--	9	67	718	11	6	1	--	811	79	160	21	23

(Table 11 continued)

County															
Ogemaw	3,431	0	15	3	2	231	581	32	–	1	–	867	97	1,387	26	10
Osceola	2,557	–	9	1	11	29	689	22	7	18	0	769	85	608	31	12
Oscoda	5,225	–	9	16	1	861	1,231	49	–	–	0	2,184	31	1,553	38	40
Otsego	4,475	–	4	31	1	284	1,153	46	1	34	1	1,555	42	799	416	29
Presque Isle	3,700	–	229	92	2	282	450	24	–	128	2	1,209	64	1,371	103	21
Roscommon	3,265	–	36	6	1	214	683	41	0	1	1	982	67	948	6	4
Wexford	7,162	–	18	1	5	182	2,907	28	7	5	1	3,153	150	1,133	127	59
Total	**124,235**	**9**	**893**	**339**	**160**	**7,133**	**28,146**	**1,203**	**78**	**438**	**38**	**38,439**	**2,846**	**31,015**	**3,478**	**757**
Southern Lower Peninsula																
Allegan	1,479	–	–	–	–	–	59	16	64	–	–	139	91	–	6	10
Barry	1,500	–	–	–	–	26	50	–	–	–	–	76	19	4	18	8
Berrien	555	–	–	–	–	–	–	–	–	–	–	–	15	–	4	3
Branch	581	–	–	–	–	–	–	–	–	–	–	–	51	–	5	4
Calhoun	909	–	–	–	–	–	–	–	32	–	–	32	90	–	31	5
Cass	475	–	–	–	–	–	4	7	–	–	–	11	13	–	4	2
Clinton	365	–	–	9	–	–	13	1	–	1	–	76	32	3	7	0
Eaton	714	–	–	–	–	144	–	–	–	–	–	144	87	1	22	19
Genesee	396	–	–	–	–	–	–	1	–	–	–	1	56	7	10	2
Gratiot	455	–	–	–	–	–	7	–	–	–	–	10	82	60	17	8
Hillsdale	410	–	–	–	–	–	–	–	–	–	–	–	18	0	6	3
Huron	260	–	–	–	–	–	0	–	–	–	–	0	33	77	2	–
Ingham	318	–	–	–	–	–	–	–	–	–	–	–	65	1	12	2
Ionia	694	–	–	–	–	30	–	0	1	–	–	31	44	2	20	34
Jackson	915	–	–	–	–	–	–	–	–	–	–	–	46	3	16	2
Kalamazoo	820	–	–	–	–	60	–	1	–	–	–	61	40	–	4	4
Kent	2,253	–	–	–	9	–	87	3	1	–	–	100	181	16	31	4
Lapeer	477	–	–	–	–	–	1	–	–	–	–	1	42	10	7	1
Lenawee	334	–	–	–	–	–	–	–	–	–	–	–	21	–	18	4
Livingston	539	–	–	–	–	–	–	0	–	0	–	0	48	2	1	0
Macomb	250	–	–	–	–	–	38	–	–	–	–	38	44	18	2	1
Monroe	114	–	–	–	–	–	–	–	–	–	–	–	28	–	1	0
Montcalm	1,498	–	–	–	–	40	123	32	1	–	–	196	119	169	19	9
Muskegon	1,928	–	–	–	29	5	659	40	–	–	–	733	24	97	4	16
Oakland	419	–	–	–	–	0	0	0	–	–	–	0	40	–	6	1
Ottawa	1,099	–	–	–	3	–	584	–	–	–	–	587	50	23	2	9
Saginaw	552	–	–	–	–	–	10	–	–	–	–	10	78	16	19	3
Sanilac	391	–	–	–	–	1	2	1	–	–	–	4	91	113	9	1
Shiawassee	169	–	–	–	–	–	1	–	–	–	–	1	41	0	9	1
St. Clair	561	1	–	–	–	–	2	2	–	–	–	4	104	5	23	1
St. Joseph	600	–	–	–	–	7	1	–	–	–	–	8	41	0	8	4
Tuscola	509	–	–	–	–	–	–	–	–	–	–	–	45	223	10	–
Van Buren	769	–	–	–	–	–	106	–	–	–	–	106	41	1	6	17
Washtenaw	410	–	–	–	–	–	–	–	–	–	–	0	22	–	4	9
Wayne	349	–	–	–	–	–	–	–	–	–	–	0	32	–	8	9
Total	**24,068**	**1**	**0**	**9**	**9**	**149**	**1,969**	**121**	**108**	**2**	–	**2,370**	**1,873**	**852**	**373**	**186**
State total	**304,258**	**10**	**4,853**	**6,066**	**3,990**	**20,631**	**38,807**	**2,909**	**186**	**8,210**	**974**	**86,636**	**6,038**	**55,744**	**6,989**	**5,904**

54

Forest Inventory Unit and county	White birch	Yellow birch	Other birch	Black cherry	Black walnut	Cotton-wood	Elm	Hickory	Hard maple	Soft maple	Red oak group	White oak group	Syca-more	Yellow-poplar	Other hardwoods	Total hardwoods
Eastern Upper Peninsula																
Alger	430	241	--	60	--	--	0	--	2,179	1,602	61	5	--	--	207	8,710
Chippewa	206	95	--	3	--	--	0	--	1,209	912	101	--	--	--	40	3,687
Delta	478	204	--	48	--	--	0	--	1,979	1,922	64	--	--	--	275	7,034
Luce	292	155	--	14	--	--	1	--	2,110	2,293	78	--	--	--	77	6,894
Mackinac	262	99	--	5	--	--	0	--	1,487	1,050	63	--	--	--	48	5,087
Menominee	269	132	--	12	--	--	1	0	1,361	1,419	184	0	--	--	774	6,159
Schoolcraft	319	148	--	18	--	--	0	--	1,342	1,441	53	--	--	--	143	5,156
Total	2,258	1,073	--	159	--	--	3	0	11,667	10,639	605	6	--	--	1,565	42,728
Western Upper Peninsula																
Baraga	434	377	--	15	--	--	1	--	2,942	2,209	129	3	--	--	657	9,469
Dickinson	281	153	2	7	--	0	1	0	1,276	1,094	98	0	--	--	1,719	6,724
Gogebic	271	264	2	55	0	3	19	7	2,220	2,473	277	8	--	--	300	7,414
Houghton	305	303	--	10	1	--	0	--	3,007	1,296	352	3	--	--	823	8,084
Iron	318	302	2	41	1	--	1	0	2,329	1,213	154	3	--	--	2,516	9,139
Keweenaw	253	200	--	9	0	--	--	3	1,280	1,334	293	3	--	--	171	4,078
Marquette	737	405	--	64	1	--	1	--	3,655	2,840	384	11	--	--	2,085	14,973
Ontonagon	291	200	--	22	--	0	1	0	1,626	1,416	172	2	--	--	1,123	7,519
Total	2,890	2,206	5	223	2	3	23	10	18,336	13,876	1,859	32	--	--	9,394	67,401
Northern Lower Peninsula																
Alcona	64	2	--	8	--	--	0	--	123	467	923	36	--	--	--	4,471
Alpena	65	5	--	0	--	--	1	--	114	448	321	19	--	0	--	2,762
Antrim	50	4	--	38	--	--	2	--	2,032	318	43	--	--	--	4	3,820
Arenac	13	0	--	1	--	11	3	0	19	242	111	24	--	--	--	784
Bay	2	--	--	0	--	2	1	0	1	103	6	22	--	--	--	270
Benzie	8	5	--	88	--	--	1	--	1,434	364	70	--	--	--	8	2,559
Charlevoix	48	11	--	6	--	--	1	--	1,029	129	37	5	--	--	1	2,205
Cheboygan	123	13	--	0	--	--	2	--	556	607	103	9	--	--	5	3,560
Clare	11	--	--	21	--	4	7	3	321	648	489	118	--	--	16	4,233
Crawford	35	0	--	11	--	--	0	--	356	706	454	75	--	--	1	3,045
Emmet	26	6	--	23	--	--	1	0	1,355	246	49	4	--	--	1	2,787
Gladwin	12	--	--	7	--	15	3	1	126	585	169	63	--	--	10	2,393
Grand Traverse	5	3	--	22	--	--	2	--	1,096	249	297	108	--	--	4	2,254
Iosco	41	0	--	2	--	43	1	0	50	517	237	29	--	--	1	1,605
Isabella	4	--	--	27	0	6	7	6	195	297	151	64	--	0	--	1,638
Kalkaska	84	2	--	68	--	--	1	--	1,460	623	194	8	--	--	0	3,759
Lake	3	--	--	29	--	0	1	--	225	281	1,151	240	--	--	13	2,575
Leelanau	10	1	--	29	1	--	6	--	1,017	152	138	1	--	--	--	1,668
Manistee	10	1	--	114	--	--	2	1	1,232	678	758	177	--	0	36	4,293
Mason	4	2	--	28	--	--	4	--	253	358	562	195	--	--	6	2,164
Mecosta	6	1	--	43	1	--	8	5	370	252	263	56	--	0	8	2,124
Midland	7	--	--	8	1	9	3	5	48	364	83	129	--	0	0	1,170
Missaukee	14	0	--	28	0	--	2	--	502	473	201	38	--	--	5	2,733
Montmorency	70	0	--	4	--	--	0	--	325	494	480	39	--	--	--	3,418
Newaygo	5	3	--	85	--	0	6	4	358	452	1,203	341	--	1	1	2,980
Oceana	1	6	--	77	2	4	5	2	314	280	355	97	--	--	1	1,427

(Table 11 continued on next page)

(Table 11 continued)

Ogemaw	23	2	--	2	--	7	3	--	159	423	379	41	--	--	3	2,564
Osceola	9	30	--	33	--	--	4	4	420	204	331	16	--	--	1	1,789
Oscoda	18	4	--	9	--	0	0	--	219	492	595	34	--	--	7	3,041
Otsego	51	6	--	12	--	--	1	--	1,103	356	86	14	--	--	5	2,920
Presque Isle	120	4	--	0	--	--	1	--	211	472	117	6	--	--	--	2,491
Roscommon	18	1	--	3	--	0	2	--	38	434	625	135	--	--	2	2,283
Wexford	5	3	--	138	--	--	9	0	1,418	428	457	54	--	--	30	4,009
Total	963	116	--	965	6	103	89	31	18,477	13,143	11,438	2,198	--	2	169	85,796
Southern Lower Peninsula																
Allegan	1	1	--	137	49	0	1	22	54	214	283	195	64	131	82	1,341
Barry	--	0	--	197	81	0	1	33	312	212	344	124	0	4	64	1,424
Berrien	0	--	--	133	5	4	4	8	169	51	56	19	17	65	2	555
Branch	--	--	--	96	62	7	2	12	62	111	98	57	1	11	0	581
Calhoun	--	--	--	234	27	4	2	42	54	182	176	25	1	2	3	877
Cass	--	0	--	200	48	0	5	20	35	49	67	13	--	7	2	464
Clinton	--	--	--	14	21	10	3	11	32	106	42	8	--	0	--	289
Eaton	--	--	--	48	23	3	6	27	150	102	53	24	--	4	0	570
Genesee	0	0	--	15	3	5	3	10	67	78	85	54	--	--	--	395
Gratiot	0	--	--	12	1	6	5	4	73	64	79	32	--	1	--	445
Hillsdale	--	--	--	71	53	2	2	10	97	27	73	45	1	2	1	410
Huron	0	0	--	3	--	38	0	0	9	47	44	5	--	--	--	260
Ingham	--	--	--	38	62	13	9	7	34	44	20	12	0	0	--	318
Ionia	--	--	--	61	83	4	3	26	113	117	109	46	--	3	--	663
Jackson	--	--	--	188	32	8	4	78	21	57	343	110	1	3	2	915
Kalamazoo	--	--	--	231	20	3	2	12	79	97	213	53	1	1	1	759
Kent	7	6	--	164	10	1	18	35	452	436	642	145	--	3	0	2,153
Lapeer	0	0	--	23	1	9	1	10	97	102	95	79	--	--	--	476
Lenawee	--	--	--	28	14	2	0	23	113	27	48	34	0	3	--	334
Livingston	--	--	--	71	1	1	65	4	10	120	161	54	--	--	0	539
Macomb	--	0	--	5	0	1	2	1	5	124	5	4	--	0	--	213
Monroe	--	--	--	3	13	4	0	9	9	28	14	4	0	0	--	114
Montcalm	4	0	--	41	3	0	8	8	105	285	366	162	--	1	0	1,301
Muskegon	0	2	--	22	3	--	0	3	82	245	581	112	--	1	3	1,195
Oakland	--	--	--	45	1	2	2	14	33	89	119	65	--	--	0	418
Ottawa	--	1	--	64	--	15	1	1	119	70	139	18	0	2	0	511
Saginaw	1	--	--	9	2	11	2	13	22	183	86	97	--	1	--	542
Sanilac	0	--	--	8	--	17	20	1	34	88	4	2	--	--	--	387
Shiawassee	--	--	--	11	3	3	1	6	13	40	26	12	--	--	--	169
St. Clair	0	2	--	7	0	70	19	5	15	164	41	97	0	--	5	557
St. Joseph	--	0	--	105	75	4	2	35	35	86	163	20	1	11	2	592
Tuscola	3	0	--	11	1	21	2	1	64	89	25	13	--	--	--	509
Van Buren	--	--	--	143	63	--	3	25	135	54	138	16	0	19	2	662
Washtenaw	--	0	--	25	70	1	2	26	25	33	92	108	--	--	--	410
Wayne	--	--	--	5	0	29	1	3	62	71	95	21	1	9	4	349
Total	18	12	--	2,470	831	296	201	545	2,791	3,892	4,924	1,887	88	284	173	21,697
State total	6,129	3,406	5	3,816	839	403	317	586	51,271	41,550	18,826	4,123	88	286	11,303	217,622

All table cells without observations are indicated by --. Table value of 0 indicates the volume rounds to less than 1 thousand cubic feet. Columns and rows may not add to their totals due to rounding.

Table 12.-- Sawtimber removals from timberland for industrial roundwood by Forest Inventory Unit, county, and species group, Michigan 2006

(In thousand board feet, International 1/4-inch rule)

Forest Inventory Unit and county	All species	Softwoods											Hardwoods			
		Eastern red-cedar	Northern white-cedar	Balsam fir	Hemlock	Jack pine	Red pine	White pine	Other pine	Spruce	Tama-rack	Total softwoods	Ash	Aspen/balsam poplar	Bass-wood	Beech
Eastern Upper Peninsula																
Alger	34,917	--	183	1,015	729	1,853	5,422	1,441	--	1,250	112	12,004	223	5,398	180	1,730
Chippewa	34,347	--	633	1,295	408	12,165	3,903	173	--	3,480	29	22,086	142	2,500	67	656
Delta	33,705	--	1,634	1,361	558	4,075	4,311	246	--	1,584	159	13,927	293	3,354	475	1,201
Luce	32,652	--	276	1,127	484	7,882	2,131	213	--	2,469	96	14,679	182	2,197	146	1,936
Mackinac	24,581	--	476	971	130	1,355	3,998	150	--	1,970	49	9,098	149	3,460	357	774
Menominee	28,215	--	3,129	1,723	877	620	1,142	204	--	1,410	371	9,476	213	3,346	874	1,058
Schoolcraft	26,815	--	441	823	250	6,763	3,880	146	--	1,240	84	13,627	168	2,210	167	1,196
Total	215,232	--	6,771	8,315	3,436	34,714	24,787	2,573	--	13,402	899	94,897	1,371	22,466	2,265	8,552
Western Upper Peninsula																
Baraga	35,344	--	206	1,020	1,112	1,850	1,334	197	--	1,379	111	7,207	404	3,951	977	1,372
Dickinson	24,844	--	390	1,325	230	1,137	1,435	490	--	2,266	322	7,595	218	4,201	1,177	504
Gogebic	25,968	--	131	551	298	34	2,264	280	--	1,524	40	5,122	737	2,211	692	250
Houghton	35,334	--	151	625	757	2,984	2,291	34	--	1,217	73	8,132	452	3,207	910	434
Iron	39,557	--	163	2,178	471	1,637	3,092	353	--	3,789	447	12,130	433	3,892	1,638	422
Keweenaw	13,891	--	143	344	129	40	168	16	--	550	21	1,410	289	485	340	328
Marquette	71,210	--	548	2,873	2,402	11,475	5,027	3,273	--	4,262	521	30,379	321	7,509	866	2,475
Ontonagon	23,879	--	256	808	837	551	1,732	351	--	1,613	82	6,229	534	5,072	735	404
Total	270,028	--	1,987	9,723	6,237	19,707	17,343	4,992	--	16,598	1,618	78,204	3,389	30,527	7,336	6,188
Northern Lower Peninsula																
Alcona	18,633	--	190	11	5	671	3,842	146	0	38	3	4,907	1,070	5,690	192	56
Alpena	12,374	9	453	88	99	231	2,292	145	2	150	6	3,476	741	3,938	196	42
Antrim	19,813	--	37	0	--	108	2,308	6	6	1	--	2,467	894	2,006	1,996	254
Arenac	3,514	2	10	0	3	434	213	68	--	0	--	730	233	868	22	21
Bay	855	--	--	--	2	4	--	5	--	--	--	12	83	223	71	--
Benzie	13,508	--	--	--	17	110	3,052	28	--	1	--	3,209	345	740	319	110
Charlevoix	11,072	--	160	14	9	1	1,631	80	--	12	9	1,917	530	1,336	1,019	204
Cheboygan	16,405	--	252	122	2	1,271	5,130	238	0	180	13	7,215	385	3,825	562	87
Clare	16,558	--	58	0	8	951	4,501	48	--	0	2	5,571	233	5,228	53	73
Crawford	21,961	--	39	4	4	4,877	8,423	129	2	22	2	13,503	53	2,625	137	39
Emmet	12,706	--	74	17	4	66	1,455	71	16	18	6	1,727	939	1,523	834	78
Gladwin	8,678	--	9	1	1	204	1,835	54	--	0	0	2,102	243	3,280	109	42
Grand Traverse	18,334	--	70	4	11	294	7,724	301	13	4	8	8,429	311	770	347	60
Iosco	19,099	6	102	22	10	2,415	11,444	223	--	16	6	14,244	228	1,593	51	15
Isabella	5,780	--	--	--	3	16	409	10	13	--	3	454	354	1,680	202	16
Kalkaska	28,877	--	58	12	24	1,411	12,753	250	18	4	2	14,533	380	2,089	1,040	202
Lake	18,204	--	60	--	11	2,325	7,503	284	2	5	2	10,193	141	1,037	100	95
Leelanau	8,572	--	--	2	37	51	783	87	1	0	5	965	505	206	278	141
Manistee	22,471	--	--	0	17	426	8,704	228	4	--	1	9,380	391	2,028	233	178
Mason	11,547	--	14	0	21	381	4,261	102	8	1	--	4,787	126	1,301	52	88
Mecosta	9,135	--	--	0	39	46	1,763	554	55	15	1	2,473	271	2,182	78	73
Midland	4,260	--	--	--	--	11	40	203	1	--	--	255	411	876	99	10
Missaukee	13,889	--	66	8	13	579	5,254	91	6	10	8	6,035	287	2,641	326	43
Montmorency	15,762	--	90	208	4	1,498	3,193	387	2	216	3	5,601	209	4,013	523	58
Newaygo	17,220	--	--	--	17	999	2,641	256	35	--	--	3,949	419	1,198	166	98
Oceana	10,007	--	--	--	22	240	3,480	50	21	3	--	3,817	342	373	78	123

(Table 12 continued)

County															
Ogemaw	11,831	2	68	8	5	1,021	2,921	135	—	4	—	4,162	418	3,907	81	19
Osceola	11,329	—	45	2	26	130	3,645	93	23	—	0	3,964	365	2,028	127	60
Oscoda	19,186	—	38	43	—	3,893	6,160	223	—	48	1	10,406	121	3,041	118	184
Otsego	17,211	—	19	82	3	1,213	5,925	177	4	90	2	7,516	175	1,804	1,124	107
Presque Isle	11,075	—	568	247	5	1,264	2,435	105	—	371	4	4,999	272	2,786	240	58
Roscommon	11,718	—	160	16	1	683	3,319	199	0	3	1	4,383	295	2,345	20	13
Wexford	27,788	—	84	2	11	670	14,103	120	21	12	2	15,026	546	2,246	438	195
Total	**469,373**	**19**	**2,725**	**915**	**442**	**28,498**	**143,144**	**5,096**	**254**	**1,227**	**89**	**182,409**	**12,317**	**71,426**	**11,230**	**2,841**
Southern Lower Peninsula																
Allegan	6,612	—	—	—	—	—	275	37	147	—	—	459	448	—	33	56
Barry	7,517	—	—	—	—	57	274	—	—	—	—	330	107	7	95	42
Berrien	2,957	—	—	—	—	—	—	—	—	—	—	—	82	—	21	17
Branch	3,070	—	—	—	—	—	—	—	—	—	—	—	280	—	28	24
Calhoun	4,402	—	—	—	—	—	21	—	73	—	—	73	442	—	157	28
Cass	2,502	—	—	24	22	—	21	41	—	—	—	63	69	—	22	11
Clinton	1,686	—	1	—	—	88	58	4	4	—	—	207	176	12	36	0
Eaton	3,753	—	—	—	—	—	826	—	—	—	—	826	428	6	115	103
Genesee	1,867	—	—	—	—	—	—	4	—	—	—	4	258	33	54	10
Gratiot	2,191	—	—	—	—	—	17	20	—	—	—	37	403	150	89	44
Hillsdale	2,192	—	—	—	—	—	—	—	—	—	—	—	97	0	29	16
Huron	1,082	—	—	—	—	—	1	—	—	—	—	1	133	267	8	—
Ingham	1,649	—	—	—	—	—	—	—	—	—	—	—	305	4	61	10
Ionia	3,624	—	—	—	—	—	168	1	5	—	—	174	240	11	104	185
Jackson	4,521	—	—	—	—	—	—	7	—	—	—	—	253	13	82	11
Kalamazoo	3,976	—	—	—	—	23	309	18	—	—	—	316	167	—	22	20
Kent	10,071	—	—	—	—	—	399	—	7	—	—	446	763	42	127	24
Lapeer	2,339	—	—	—	—	—	3	—	18	—	—	3	180	44	36	7
Lenawee	1,804	—	—	—	—	—	—	—	—	—	—	—	117	—	91	21
Livingston	2,269	—	—	—	—	—	—	1	21	—	—	1	215	7	4	0
Macomb	884	—	—	—	—	—	216	—	—	—	—	216	171	29	8	3
Monroe	513	—	—	—	—	—	—	—	—	—	—	—	102	—	3	1
Montcalm	6,755	—	—	—	—	92	618	114	4	—	—	828	582	456	91	49
Muskegon	9,196	—	—	—	—	135	3,695	147	18	—	—	3,995	112	187	12	76
Oakland	1,882	—	—	—	—	—	2	2	—	—	—	2	171	5	32	5
Ottawa	5,936	—	—	—	—	7	3,354	1	—	—	—	3,363	223	104	12	48
Saginaw	2,697	—	—	—	—	—	6	27	21	—	—	54	375	75	99	14
Sanilac	1,618	—	—	—	—	3	6	3	—	—	—	12	502	199	34	6
Shiawassee	853	—	—	—	—	—	4	—	—	—	—	4	227	2	48	6
St. Clair	2,935	4	—	—	—	—	9	9	—	—	—	22	569	23	118	5
St. Joseph	3,173	—	—	—	—	—	6	41	—	—	—	47	227	1	39	20
Tuscola	2,014	—	—	—	—	—	—	—	—	—	—	—	196	730	54	3
Van Buren	4,152	—	—	—	—	—	612	—	—	—	—	612	226	—	29	96
Washtenaw	1,952	—	—	—	—	—	—	2	—	—	—	2	120	4	22	—
Wayne	1,646	—	—	—	—	—	—	—	0	—	—	0	160	—	39	46
Total	**116,287**	**4**	**1**	**24**	**22**	**404**	**10,877**	**481**	**276**	**6**		**12,099**	**9,128**	**2,406**	**1,854**	**1,008**
State total	**1,070,920**	**23**	**11,484**	**18,978**	**10,137**	**83,324**	**196,150**	**13,141**	**530**	**2,609**	**6**	**367,609**	**26,204**	**126,826**	**22,685**	**18,589**

Forest Inventory Unit and county	White birch	Yellow birch	Other birch	Black cherry	Black walnut	Cotton-wood	Elm	Hickory	Hard maple	Soft maple	Red oak group	White oak group	Syca-more	Yellow-poplar	Other hardwoods	Total hardwoods
Eastern Upper Peninsula																
Alger	1,235	1,034	--	306	--	--	1	--	9,017	3,328	129	28	--	--	303	22,913
Chippewa	588	378	--	13	--	--	0	--	5,224	2,210	424	--	--	--	59	12,261
Delta	1,326	786	--	245	--	--	1	--	7,355	4,231	108	--	--	--	403	19,778
Luce	626	581	--	72	--	--	2	--	7,529	4,388	202	--	--	--	112	17,973
Mackinac	834	379	--	27	--	--	0	--	6,598	2,626	206	--	--	--	71	15,483
Menominee	740	544	--	62	--	--	3	0	5,610	4,321	836	0	--	--	1,133	18,739
Schoolcraft	777	555	--	90	--	--	0	--	4,658	3,055	102	--	--	--	209	13,188
Total	6,126	4,258	--	815	--	--	6	0	45,990	24,158	2,008	28	--	--	2,289	120,335
Western Upper Peninsula																
Baraga	925	1,699	--	74	--	--	1	--	12,186	5,058	411	15	--	--	1,064	28,137
Dickinson	775	631	9	36	--	0	2	0	4,841	2,002	340	0	--	--	2,514	17,250
Gogebic	483	1,140	9	284	2	4	27	26	8,937	4,410	1,124	32	--	--	478	20,846
Houghton	695	1,322	--	49	3	--	0	--	13,642	3,554	1,366	17	--	--	1,550	27,202
Iron	1,091	1,496	8	213	3	--	2	0	10,764	3,017	699	13	--	--	3,737	27,427
Keweenaw	665	855	--	46	1	--	--	14	4,714	3,208	1,272	13	--	--	250	12,480
Marquette	1,930	1,752	--	326	4	--	1	--	14,622	6,167	1,768	40	--	--	3,049	40,831
Ontonagon	473	685	--	115	--	0	2	1	5,045	2,604	268	11	--	--	1,701	17,650
Total	7,036	9,581	25	1,144	13	5	35	42	74,750	30,019	7,248	143	--	--	14,342	191,824
Northern Lower Peninsula																
Alcona	166	11	--	39	--	--	2	--	565	1,215	4,547	174	--	--	--	13,726
Alpena	197	25	--	2	--	--	4	--	517	1,527	1,615	92	--	3	--	8,898
Antrim	78	18	--	192	--	1	6	--	10,756	919	222	--	--	--	6	17,346
Arenac	38	1	--	4	--	53	12	0	81	799	533	118	--	--	--	2,784
Bay	5	--	--	0	--	10	3	0	3	315	32	98	--	--	--	843
Benzie	22	14	--	441	--	--	3	--	7,046	907	345	--	--	--	8	10,299
Charlevoix	198	34	--	28	--	--	2	--	5,053	558	168	24	--	--	1	9,155
Cheboygan	243	47	--	2	--	--	5	--	2,323	1,190	471	43	--	--	7	9,190
Clare	33	--	--	87	--	19	19	11	1,169	1,745	1,833	459	--	--	24	10,986
Crawford	64	0	--	59	--	--	0	--	1,614	1,335	2,176	356	--	--	--	8,458
Emmet	62	25	--	117	--	--	3	1	6,464	684	226	22	--	--	2	10,979
Gladwin	49	--	--	23	--	72	9	6	394	1,387	668	280	--	--	14	6,576
Grand Traverse	17	9	--	111	--	--	6	--	5,637	784	1,385	463	--	4	--	9,905
Iosco	102	0	--	11	--	223	3	0	225	1,157	1,109	138	--	--	--	4,854
Isabella	14	--	--	138	1	26	22	30	958	940	643	301	--	0	2	5,326
Kalkaska	151	7	--	352	--	--	2	--	7,534	1,597	951	37	--	--	0	14,344
Lake	7	--	--	135	--	1	3	--	789	736	4,185	763	--	--	19	8,011
Leelanau	30	2	--	149	3	--	18	--	5,074	581	620	3	--	--	--	7,607
Manistee	29	3	--	538	--	--	5	3	4,480	1,971	2,601	598	--	0	33	13,092
Mason	10	5	--	133	--	0	9	--	1,038	1,223	2,071	698	--	--	7	6,761
Mecosta	17	3	--	210	6	--	24	19	1,562	767	1,174	263	--	--	11	6,661
Midland	24	--	--	41	8	44	9	23	246	1,241	404	568	--	2	0	4,005
Missaukee	36	7	--	136	1	--	5	--	2,204	1,167	839	155	--	2	7	7,854
Montmorency	145	1	--	21	--	--	0	--	1,391	1,279	2,333	188	--	--	--	10,161
Newaygo	14	10	--	435	--	1	16	20	1,920	1,919	5,616	1,433	--	4	3	13,271
Oceana	4	20	--	394	12	18	12	10	1,658	1,106	1,646	391	--	--	2	6,190

(Table 12 continued on next page)

(Table 12 continued)

County																Total
Ogemaw	84	4	--	8	--	23	11	--	539	958	1,488	127	--	--	3	7,669
Osceola	27	110	--	170	--	--	10	22	2,069	794	1,513	68	--	--	2	7,365
Oscoda	59	19	--	38	--	0	0	--	969	1,189	2,877	154	--	--	10	8,780
Otsego	130	21	--	59	--	4	4	--	5,008	817	374	64	--	--	8	9,695
Presque Isle	270	18	--	1	--	3	3	--	882	961	555	29	--	--	--	6,076
Roscommon	61	3	--	14	--	6	6	--	142	1,065	2,779	588	--	--	3	7,335
Wexford	14	8	--	673	--	1	23	2	6,231	957	1,281	103	--	--	43	12,761
Total	2,399	425	--	4,758	31	493	260	148	86,539	35,789	49,281	8,795	--	11	220	286,964
Southern Lower Peninsula																
Allegan	5	5	--	659	271	0	4	119	305	920	1,383	930	149	673	193	6,153
Barry	--	0	--	1,013	447	1	3	179	1,765	1,043	1,703	601	0	23	160	7,187
Berrien	0	--	--	685	29	21	21	46	957	261	290	97	85	334	9	2,957
Branch	--	--	--	493	338	36	11	66	352	570	512	294	6	55	4	3,070
Calhoun	--	--	--	1,157	150	23	12	231	306	801	866	131	3	10	10	4,328
Cass	--	1	--	1,027	262	0	29	108	196	251	348	68	--	36	11	2,439
Clinton	--	--	--	72	116	49	18	58	180	500	220	41	--	0	--	1,479
Eaton	--	--	--	247	126	13	32	150	850	436	275	125	--	20	0	2,926
Genesee	0	0	--	75	15	24	15	57	379	311	395	236	--	--	--	1,863
Gratiot	2	--	--	61	6	32	24	22	412	326	411	168	--	6	--	2,154
Hillsdale	--	--	--	363	291	8	9	57	548	140	380	234	6	9	4	2,192
Huron	1	0	--	15	--	194	3	0	53	195	183	28	--	--	--	1,081
Ingham	--	--	--	197	342	66	44	38	190	224	103	64	0	0	--	1,649
Ionia	--	--	--	314	455	18	13	140	641	511	564	240	--	14	--	3,450
Jackson	--	--	--	923	176	39	21	378	121	247	1,693	533	3	18	10	4,521
Kalamazoo	--	--	--	1,137	109	14	12	66	447	407	1,013	229	5	6	4	3,660
Kent	36	14	--	797	55	5	60	164	2,328	1,709	2,875	605	--	16	2	9,624
Lapeer	0	0	--	117	7	47	4	54	551	478	447	365	--	--	--	2,336
Lenawee	--	--	--	145	77	11	2	126	637	138	247	178	1	13	--	1,804
Livingston	--	--	--	320	7	7	152	24	58	390	796	286	--	--	1	2,268
Macomb	--	1	--	23	0	5	5	6	28	343	27	18	--	0	--	668
Monroe	--	--	--	16	69	22	0	51	53	100	70	21	0	1	--	513
Montcalm	20	2	--	212	16	1	36	44	580	1,275	1,777	777	--	8	0	5,926
Muskegon	0	11	--	112	19	--	1	17	375	1,005	2,755	509	--	6	4	5,201
Oakland	--	--	--	187	7	9	12	75	184	369	530	296	--	--	2	1,880
Ottawa	--	3	--	328	--	75	7	5	670	313	682	92	0	8	2	2,573
Saginaw	5	--	--	47	13	58	10	70	122	848	401	503	--	4	--	2,643
Sanilac	2	--	--	39	--	85	105	3	195	407	20	12	--	--	--	1,607
Shiawassee	--	--	--	58	19	14	7	33	74	160	137	65	--	--	--	849
St. Clair	1	8	--	34	0	7	96	30	88	839	213	501	1	--	24	2,912
St. Joseph	--	1	--	540	414	361	8	194	195	440	847	103	6	59	7	3,126
Tuscola	17	0	--	54	5	22	194	8	364	271	130	68	--	--	--	2,014
Van Buren	--	--	--	737	347	105	8	15	764	276	719	85	2	98	9	3,540
Washtenaw	--	0	--	131	336	--	15	137	144	125	384	527	--	--	--	1,950
Wayne	--	--	--	25	2	139	11	140	323	306	423	101	3	44	18	1,646
Total	88	48	--	12,363	4,528	1,508	2,910	815	15,437	16,934	23,821	9,134	271	1,461	475	104,188
State total	15,650	14,310	25	19,080	4,572	2,006	3,100	1,115	222,717	106,900	82,357	18,100	271	1,472	17,327	703,311

All table cells without observations are indicated by --. Table value of 0 indicates the volume rounds to less than 1 thousand board feet. Columns and rows may not add to their totals due to rounding.

Table 13.-- Harvest residue generated by industrial roundwood harvesting by Forest Inventory Unit, county, and species group, Michigan, 2006

(In thousand cubic feet)

Forest Inventory Unit and county	All species	Softwoods											Hardwoods			
		Eastern red-cedar	Northern white-cedar	Balsam fir	Hemlock	Jack pine	Red pine	White pine	Other pine	Spruce	Tamarack	Total softwoods	Ash	Aspen/balsam poplar	Basswood	Beech
Eastern Upper Peninsula																
Alger	3,966	--	20	120	114	201	346	90	--	132	15	1,039	34	750	23	268
Chippewa	3,450	--	64	151	64	1,207	257	19	--	369	4	2,134	20	207	9	113
Delta	4,044	--	191	166	87	425	301	28	--	171	21	1,390	41	345	44	269
Luce	4,237	--	33	141	76	840	147	21	--	280	13	1,551	36	265	18	347
Mackinac	2,543	--	50	110	20	163	267	18	--	201	6	836	22	398	28	124
Menominee	3,242	--	364	216	138	85	106	26	--	163	49	1,147	23	323	81	183
Schoolcraft	3,232	--	47	98	39	684	275	14	--	129	11	1,298	29	270	28	216
Total	24,714	--	770	1,003	539	3,605	1,699	216	--	1,444	118	9,394	206	2,558	231	1,519
Western Upper Peninsula																
Baraga	4,268	--	20	119	168	194	105	17	--	151	15	790	53	447	78	330
Dickinson	3,152	--	45	161	36	129	124	38	--	247	42	822	30	390	131	121
Gogebic	3,104	--	13	59	42	5	134	17	--	151	5	426	102	243	72	57
Houghton	3,694	--	17	70	115	303	176	4	--	119	10	813	66	356	88	104
Iron	4,355	--	19	262	71	191	251	34	--	432	59	1,319	51	395	127	101
Keweenaw	1,732	--	14	36	20	6	14	2	--	54	3	149	43	55	33	76
Marquette	8,438	--	60	352	377	1,197	377	212	--	458	68	3,100	46	862	79	557
Ontonagon	3,370	--	33	88	127	60	116	24	--	161	11	620	91	526	94	97
Total	32,113	--	220	1,147	956	2,085	1,297	348	--	1,773	212	8,038	480	3,274	701	1,444
Northern Lower Peninsula																
Alcona	1,388	--	21	0	0	72	224	7	0	2	0	326	59	591	15	7
Alpena	943	1	53	10	6	24	131	8	0	16	0	248	43	363	20	8
Antrim	1,355	4	4	0	--	12	138	0	--	0	--	155	54	147	147	21
Arenac	253	0	1	0	0	45	12	3	--	0	--	61	12	67	3	2
Bay	61	--	--	--	--	1	--	0	--	--	--	1	4	21	4	--
Benzie	873	--	--	--	0	16	183	1	--	0	--	201	18	82	19	7
Charlevoix	768	--	16	1	0	0	93	4	0	0	0	114	27	107	88	12
Cheboygan	1,456	--	25	13	0	138	298	11	0	19	0	505	30	399	61	17
Clare	1,404	--	6	0	0	99	265	2	1	0	0	373	18	565	5	15
Crawford	1,791	--	4	0	0	489	504	6	0	0	0	1,006	6	299	19	5
Emmet	942	--	7	1	1	10	90	3	1	1	0	113	52	138	65	9
Gladwin	770	--	1	0	0	25	108	3	0	0	0	136	20	299	7	9
Grand Traverse	1,075	--	7	0	0	31	451	14	1	0	0	505	16	64	20	4
Iosco	1,343	1	10	2	1	247	667	11	1	1	0	939	14	140	4	4
Isabella	403	--	--	--	0	2	25	0	1	--	0	29	16	166	10	2
Kalkaska	2,025	--	6	1	1	153	761	12	1	0	0	935	27	208	76	18
Lake	1,226	--	6	--	0	224	433	14	0	0	0	677	15	115	7	14
Leelanau	465	--	--	0	1	6	45	3	0	0	0	55	23	21	15	7
Manistee	1,297	--	--	0	0	53	538	10	0	0	0	601	22	101	14	11
Mason	642	--	1	0	0	40	248	5	0	0	--	295	8	72	3	7
Mecosta	640	--	--	0	3	7	108	31	3	0	0	153	18	209	5	9
Midland	272	--	--	--	--	2	4	9	0	--	--	15	19	83	6	1
Missaukee	1,083	--	6	0	4	61	316	4	0	0	0	389	17	283	37	6
Montmorency	1,315	--	9	25	0	147	185	26	0	26	0	419	20	395	62	12
Newaygo	920	--	--	--	0	94	160	13	3	--	--	271	20	86	9	6
Oceana	561	--	--	--	0	26	204	3	2	0	--	235	17	35	4	7
Ogemaw	872	0	7	0	0	101	174	7	0	0	--	289	21	322	6	2
Osceola	642	--	4	0	1	12	209	5	1	--	0	232	18	139	7	4

(Table 13 continued)

County																
Oscoda	1,551	—	—	—	—	—	382	372	15	—	5	0	783	13	355	11	16
Otsego	1,393	—	—	2	10	0	121	352	12	0	11	0	508	16	181	116	15
Presque Isle	1,066	—	—	62	28	0	124	144	7	—	44	0	409	24	313	28	13
Roscommon	799	—	—	16	1	0	79	193	11	0	0	0	299	16	218	1	2
Wexford	1,998	—	—	8	0	1	69	823	6	1	0	0	908	48	242	26	30
Total	33,593	2	0	285	97	17	2,911	8,459	267	16	131	2	12,187	753	6,826	918	300
Southern Lower Peninsula																	
Allegan	321	—	—	—	—	—	—	15	1	3	—	—	19	23	—	2	3
Barry	409	—	—	—	—	8	—	17	—	—	—	—	25	6	1	6	2
Berrien	174	—	—	—	—	—	—	—	—	—	—	—	—	4	—	1	1
Branch	164	—	—	—	—	—	—	—	—	—	—	—	—	15	—	2	1
Calhoun	229	—	—	—	—	—	—	—	2	2	—	—	2	22	—	9	1
Cass	140	—	—	—	—	—	—	1	—	—	—	—	4	4	—	1	1
Clinton	105	—	—	0	3	13	—	4	0	—	1	0	26	9	1	2	0
Eaton	204	—	—	—	—	—	—	48	—	—	—	—	48	21	0	7	5
Genesee	94	—	—	—	—	—	—	—	0	—	—	—	0	12	2	3	1
Gratiot	123	—	—	—	—	—	—	3	1	1	—	—	4	20	14	5	2
Hillsdale	118	—	—	—	—	—	—	—	—	—	—	—	—	5	0	2	1
Huron	60	—	—	—	—	—	—	0	—	—	—	—	0	—	19	4	—
Ingham	89	—	—	—	—	—	—	—	0	—	—	—	—	15	0	—	1
Ionia	191	—	—	—	—	—	—	10	0	0	—	—	10	13	1	6	10
Jackson	223	—	—	—	—	—	—	—	—	—	—	—	—	13	1	5	1
Kalamazoo	203	—	—	—	—	—	—	17	0	—	—	—	18	8	—	1	1
Kent	506	—	—	—	—	1	—	21	1	1	—	—	24	35	4	6	1
Lapeer	122	—	—	—	—	—	—	0	—	—	—	—	0	8	3	2	0
Lenawee	99	—	—	—	—	—	—	—	—	—	—	—	—	6	—	5	0
Livingston	102	—	—	—	—	—	—	—	0	—	—	—	0	10	0	5	0
Macomb	41	—	—	—	—	—	—	13	—	—	—	—	13	7	4	0	0
Monroe	25	—	—	—	—	—	—	—	—	—	—	—	—	4	—	0	0
Montcalm	375	—	—	—	—	13	—	35	5	0	—	—	53	30	39	6	3
Muskegon	511	—	—	—	—	13	—	211	6	1	—	—	232	8	22	1	6
Oakland	91	—	—	—	—	—	—	—	0	—	—	—	0	8	—	2	—
Ottawa	337	—	—	—	—	1	—	194	0	—	—	—	195	11	6	1	3
Saginaw	138	—	—	—	—	—	—	0	2	2	—	—	4	19	4	6	1
Sanilac	110	—	—	—	—	0	—	1	0	—	—	—	2	26	26	3	0
Shiawassee	44	—	—	—	—	—	—	0	—	—	—	—	0	12	0	3	0
St. Clair	158	0	—	—	—	—	—	1	1	—	—	—	1	30	1	7	0
St. Joseph	169	—	—	—	—	—	—	0	2	—	—	—	3	12	—	2	0
Tuscola	134	—	—	—	—	—	—	—	—	—	—	—	—	9	55	3	7
Van Buren	231	—	—	—	—	—	—	35	—	—	—	—	35	12	—	2	—
Washtenaw	96	—	—	—	—	—	—	—	0	—	—	—	0	6	0	1	2
Wayne	81	—	—	—	—	—	—	—	—	0	—	—	0	8	—	2	2
Total	6,215	0	0	3	3	50	—	627	23	9	1	0	718	459	205	110	56
State total	96,635	3	0	1,275	2,250	1,516	8,652	12,081	854	25	3,348	332	30,336	1,899	12,862	1,961	3,320

		Hardwoods														
Forest Inventory Unit and county	White birch	Yellow birch	Other birch	Black cherry	Black walnut	Cotton-wood	Elm	Hickory	Hard maple	Soft maple	Red oak group	White oak group	Syca-more	Yellow-poplar	Other hardwoods	Total hardwoods
Eastern Upper Peninsula																
Alger	128	106	--	18	--	--	0	--	1,057	467	15	1	--	--	60	2,927
Chippewa	61	45	--	1	--	--	0	--	558	267	23	--	--	--	12	1,316
Delta	143	101	--	15	--	--	0	--	1,040	562	15	--	--	--	79	2,654
Luce	86	78	--	4	--	--	0	--	1,145	667	18	--	--	--	22	2,686
Mackinac	81	48	--	2	--	--	0	--	668	308	14	--	--	--	14	1,707
Menominee	80	60	--	4	--	--	0	0	656	421	41	0	--	--	223	2,096
Schoolcraft	95	75	--	5	--	--	0	--	742	421	12	--	--	--	41	1,934
Total	674	513	--	49	--	--	1	0	5,866	3,113	138	1	--	--	452	15,320
Western Upper Peninsula																
Baraga	128	156	--	4	--	--	0	--	1,415	647	30	1	--	--	190	3,478
Dickinson	85	72	1	2	--	0	0	0	660	318	25	0	--	--	496	2,330
Gogebic	79	117	1	17	0	1	5	4	1,102	718	71	2	--	--	87	2,678
Houghton	91	133	--	3	0	--	0	0	1,324	383	92	1	--	--	239	2,881
Iron	97	111	0	13	0	--	0	0	1,010	358	47	1	--	--	726	3,036
Keweenaw	81	92	--	3	0	--	--	1	682	391	77	1	--	--	49	1,583
Marquette	223	182	--	20	0	--	0	--	1,826	831	108	2	--	--	602	5,338
Ontonagon	84	110	--	7	--	0	0	0	961	412	43	1	--	--	324	2,751
Total	867	973	2	69	1	1	7	5	8,980	4,059	493	7	--	--	2,714	24,075
Northern Lower Peninsula																
Alcona	17	1	--	2	--	--	0	--	48	129	187	7	--	--	--	1,062
Alpena	18	1	--	0	--	0	0	--	44	127	67	4	--	0	--	695
Antrim	14	1	--	12	--	--	1	--	701	93	10	--	--	--	1	1,200
Arenac	3	0	--	0	--	3	1	0	9	65	22	5	--	--	--	191
Bay	0	--	--	0	--	1	0	0	0	24	1	4	--	--	--	60
Benzie	1	0	--	26	--	--	0	--	421	82	14	--	--	--	1	672
Charlevoix	10	1	--	2	--	--	0	--	363	35	7	1	--	--	0	654
Cheboygan	33	5	--	0	--	--	0	--	218	167	20	2	--	--	1	951
Clare	1	--	--	6	--	1	1	--	153	151	87	21	--	--	5	1,031
Crawford	10	0	--	4	--	--	0	--	139	201	88	14	--	--	--	785
Emmet	6	2	--	7	--	--	0	--	471	68	10	1	--	--	--	828
Gladwin	3	--	--	2	--	4	0	0	73	166	35	13	--	--	3	634
Grand Traverse	1	0	--	7	--	--	0	0	327	57	56	18	--	--	0	570
Iosco	11	0	--	1	--	13	0	0	22	145	45	6	--	--	0	404
Isabella	1	--	--	8	0	1	1	1	57	70	28	13	--	0	0	374
Kalkaska	23	0	--	21	--	--	0	--	501	175	39	1	--	--	0	1,090
Lake	0	--	--	9	--	0	0	--	114	66	175	30	--	--	4	549
Leelanau	1	0	--	9	0	--	0	--	275	33	25	0	--	--	--	410
Manistee	1	0	--	32	--	--	1	--	259	123	107	24	--	0	2	696
Mason	0	0	--	8	--	0	0	0	72	65	84	26	--	--	1	347
Mecosta	1	0	--	13	0	--	1	1	117	52	47	11	--	0	2	487
Midland	1	--	--	2	0	3	0	0	16	85	17	22	--	0	0	257
Missaukee	1	0	--	8	0	--	0	--	190	110	35	6	--	--	1	694
Montmorency	20	0	--	1	--	--	0	--	142	139	97	8	--	--	--	896
Newaygo	0	0	--	26	--	0	1	--	109	106	228	56	--	0	--	649
Oceana	0	1	--	24	1	1	0	--	97	59	66	14	--	--	0	326
Ogemaw	5	0	--	0	--	1	0	--	43	111	65	6	--	--	0	583
Osceola	1	5	--	10	--	--	0	1	117	42	62	3	--	--	0	410

(Table 13 continued on next page)

(Table 13 continued)

															Total
Oscoda	5	1	—	3	—	0	—	0	95	141	122	7	—	2	768
Otsego	14	2	—	4	—	0	—	0	418	98	15	3	—	2	884
Presque Isle	32	1	—	0	—	0	1	—	89	132	23	1	—	—	657
Roscommon	3	0	—	1	—	0	—	0	20	106	109	23	—	1	500
Wexford	0	0	—	42	—	1	0	—	495	106	82	10	—	8	1,090
Total	237	24	—	293	2	9	7	28	6,214	3,326	2,073	357	—	36	21,406
Southern Lower Peninsula															
Allegan	0	0	—	38	14	0	6	0	18	49	59	41	3	4	302
Barry	—	0	—	61	24	0	10	0	109	61	73	26	0	3	384
Berrien	0	—	—	42	2	1	2	1	61	16	12	4	5	1	174
Branch	—	—	—	29	18	2	4	1	20	34	22	12	0	0	164
Calhoun	—	—	—	68	8	1	12	1	18	44	36	6	0	1	227
Cass	—	0	—	62	14	0	6	2	12	15	15	3	—	1	136
Clinton	—	—	—	4	6	3	3	0	10	28	9	2	—	0	79
Eaton	—	—	—	15	7	1	8	1	48	23	12	5	1	0	156
Genesee	0	0	—	4	1	1	3	0	24	16	16	9	—	1	93
Gratiot	0	—	—	4	0	2	1	1	24	19	17	7	0	0	119
Hillsdale	—	—	—	22	16	0	3	0	34	8	16	10	1	1	118
Huron	0	0	—	1	—	12	0	12	3	10	7	1	0	0	60
Ingham	—	—	—	12	18	4	2	4	11	13	4	3	0	0	89
Ionia	—	—	—	19	24	1	7	3	37	28	24	10	1	1	181
Jackson	—	—	—	54	10	2	19	1	7	13	71	24	0	1	223
Kalamazoo	—	—	—	67	6	1	4	1	26	21	41	9	0	0	186
Kent	2	0	—	47	3	0	8	2	139	83	123	25	—	1	481
Lapeer	0	0	—	7	0	3	3	3	35	27	18	15	—	0	122
Lenawee	—	—	—	9	4	1	7	1	39	8	10	7	0	1	99
Livingston	—	—	—	18	0	0	1	0	3	16	34	14	—	1	102
Macomb	—	0	—	1	0	3	0	0	2	11	1	1	—	—	29
Monroe	—	—	—	1	4	1	3	1	3	5	3	1	0	0	25
Montcalm	—	0	—	13	1	0	2	0	33	80	78	34	0	1	323
Muskegon	0	1	—	7	1	2	1	1	34	58	119	20	—	0	279
Oakland	—	—	—	10	0	1	4	1	10	19	22	13	0	—	90
Ottawa	—	0	—	20	—	4	0	0	44	17	31	4	—	1	142
Saginaw	0	—	—	3	1	3	4	0	7	48	16	22	0	0	134
Sanilac	0	—	—	2	—	5	6	1	11	27	1	1	—	—	108
Shiawassee	—	—	—	3	1	1	0	2	8	8	6	3	—	—	44
St. Clair	0	0	—	2	0	22	2	6	5	50	9	21	0	1	157
St. Joseph	—	0	—	32	24	1	10	1	12	26	36	4	0	—	166
Tuscola	1	0	—	3	0	6	0	0	23	22	5	3	—	4	134
Van Buren	—	—	—	44	18	—	7	1	46	17	32	4	—	1	196
Washtenaw	—	0	—	8	18	0	7	0	8	6	15	25	0	6	96
Wayne	—	—	—	1	0	7	0	1	17	15	19	5	0	—	81
Total	5	2	—	731	244	89	153	89	937	942	1,011	395	11	88	5,497
State total	1,783	1,512	2	1,142	247	59	165	118	21,997	11,440	3,716	760	11	89	66,298

All table cells without observations are indicated by — . Table value of 0 indicates the volume rounds to less than 1 thousand cubic feet. Columns and rows may not add to their totals due to rounding.

Table 14. -- Disposition of residues produced at primary wood-using mills by Forest Inventory Unit, disposition, residue type, and softwoods and hardwoods, Michigan, 2006

(In thousand tons, green weight)

Forest Inventory Unit and disposition	Total all residues		Residue type							
			Total wood residue		Wood residue				Bark	
					Coarse		Fine			
	Softwood	Hardwood	Softwood	Hardwood	Softwood	Hardwood	Softwood	Hardwood	Softwood	Hardwood
All Units										
Fiber products	545.61	399.68	545.61	395.38	411.94	374.08	133.67	21.30	--	4.30
Industrial fuel used at mill	138.97	630.65	51.61	248.39	1.60	30.48	50.02	217.91	87.36	382.26
Industrial fuel-sold	150.78	438.42	93.56	238.25	29.24	118.02	64.32	120.23	57.22	200.17
Domestic fuel	4.04	51.88	3.13	36.19	3.13	33.37	--	2.82	0.91	15.69
Miscellaneous[a]	188.48	378.27	67.01	190.16	18.40	55.42	48.61	134.74	121.47	188.11
Not used	15.51	8.30	15.12	6.04	0.32	2.35	14.80	3.70	0.39	2.26
Total	1,043.39	1,907.21	776.05	1,114.42	464.63	613.72	311.42	500.71	267.34	792.79
Eastern Upper Peninsula										
Fiber products	12.52	85.72	12.52	85.72	12.52	84.82	--	0.90	--	--
Industrial fuel used at mill	75.94	202.35	27.18	75.92	0.09	8.67	27.09	67.25	48.76	126.43
Industrial fuel-sold	6.15	38.51	1.56	24.96	0.39	4.90	1.16	20.05	4.59	13.55
Domestic fuel	0.16	10.70	0.10	2.17	0.10	0.99	--	1.18	0.06	8.53
Miscellaneous[a]	22.30	32.23	15.12	5.07	6.00	1.41	9.12	3.66	7.18	27.16
Not used	0.04	0.41	0.03	0.33	0.02	0.18	0.01	0.15	0.01	0.08
Total	117.09	369.91	56.50	194.17	19.11	100.97	37.39	93.19	60.59	175.74
Western Upper Peninsula										
Fiber products	307.52	108.63	307.52	108.63	215.38	108.63	92.13	--	--	--
Industrial fuel used at mill	43.03	321.40	10.39	125.23	--	0.23	10.39	125.00	32.64	196.17
Industrial fuel-sold	49.02	163.68	9.46	48.19	1.88	7.10	7.58	41.09	39.56	115.49
Domestic fuel	0.09	--	0.07	--	0.07	--	--	--	0.02	--
Miscellaneous[a]	46.29	16.02	24.91	10.18	0.22	0.03	24.69	10.14	21.38	5.84
Total	445.95	609.71	352.35	292.22	217.56	115.99	134.80	176.23	93.60	317.49

(Table 14 continued on next page)

(Table 14 continued)

Northern Lower Peninsula

Fiber products	225.57	147.13	225.57	142.83	184.04	122.42	41.54	20.40	4.30
Industrial fuel used at mill	19.61	84.95	13.66	25.97	1.14	6.65	12.51	19.31	5.95
Industrial fuel-sold	95.62	203.67	82.54	132.63	26.96	75.82	55.58	56.81	13.08
Domestic fuel	3.63	31.26	2.85	26.10	2.85	24.45	--	1.65	5.16
Miscellaneous[a]	119.60	210.88	26.83	107.44	12.15	31.30	14.68	76.14	103.44
Not used	15.31	3.44	14.97	3.35	0.20	0.21	14.77	3.13	0.09
Total	479.34	681.33	366.42	438.32	227.34	260.87	139.08	177.45	243.01

Southern Lower Peninsula

Fiber products	--	58.21	--	58.21	--	58.21	--	--	--
Industrial fuel used at mill	0.38	21.95	0.38	21.27	0.37	14.93	0.02	6.35	0.68
Industrial fuel-sold	--	32.58	--	32.48	--	30.20	--	2.28	0.10
Domestic fuel	0.17	9.94	0.12	7.93	0.12	7.93	--	--	2.01
Miscellaneous[a]	0.29	119.14	0.15	67.47	0.03	22.67	0.12	44.80	51.67
Not used	0.16	4.46	0.12	2.36	0.10	1.95	0.02	0.41	2.10
Total	1.00	246.28	0.77	189.72	0.62	135.89	0.16	53.83	56.56

[a] Livestock bedding, mulch, small dimension, and specialty items,

All table cells without observations are indicated by -- . Columns and rows may not add to their totals due to rounding.